Turn off the computer. Turn off every appliance in your house. Unplug them all. Take out all the batteries from every electronic device. You want to be the only source of energy in the room.

ALBUMS BY NICK JAINA

*Primary Perception*
*The Beanstalks That Have Brought Us Here Are Gone*
*A Bird in the Opera House*
*A Narrow Way*
*Wool*
*The Seven Stations*
*The Bluff of All Time*

Sutton, AK
7.29.16

NICK JAINA

# *Get It While You Can*

Dear Lily,

This is a book about invisibility.

Enjoy,

a Perfect Day book


Parts of this book appeared in very different forms in *Satellite Press Transmission, Eye Rhyme, Somnambulist, fields, Willamette Week, Oregon Humanities, Under the Gum Tree, Portland Mercury,* and *McSweeney's Quarterly.*



Get It While You Can / Nick Jaina
ISBN: 978-0-9836327-4-0
Library of Congress Control Number: 2014955293

Second printing 2016

Cover design by Aaron Robert Miller
Photograph by Michelle Christiance
Illustrations by Sean Hayashi
Perfect Day logo by Corinne Manning
Copyedited by Lydia Mazer
Website by David Small

Printed by Worzalla in the United States of America
Set in Garamond & Hoefler Text at the IPRC

www.nickjaina.com
www.perfectdaypublishing.com

"I teach one thing and one thing only: that is, suffering and the end of suffering."

-Gautama Buddha

# *Get It While You Can*

# *One*

I AM STARING out the window at an orange kite hanging in the air. Its long tail is fluttering in the wind, but for a solid minute now the diamond of the kite body has stayed motionless in the sky, almost as if it were pinned there. From my angle I can't see the person holding the kite, and I'm much too far away to see the string. Just now the unseen person has decided to let out more line. At first, the kite shudders, like a sick dog trying to back out of one of those horrible neck cones, and then it accepts its new directive and rises out of view.

To sum up: I am looking out the window at a person flying a kite, but I can't see the person, or the kite, or the string. I see nothing.

For a long time I thought music was the thing that would ground me. I still believe that in some ways, but what I have been caught up in lately is this: I feel that I am good at writing a song, at being able to play guitar, at all the various skills that go into making a record, and yet for many years I have had the strong feeling that I have failed at music. Worse yet, I feel that since I have devoted my life to music, I have failed at life.

I came to the Oregon coast because I want to learn how to sail. A young man named Daniel is my teacher. He is working at an Irish pub in town while helping his friend prepare his twenty-nine foot fiberglass full keel sailboat for a long sea voyage. In the spring the two of them are going to try to sail it to Hawaii.

Last night, walking me along the shore, Daniel talked about the basics of sailing with the kind of enthusiasm that comes from being in the middle of learning about it himself. He told me about how the golden arcs on Earth give you the most direct line to a destination. He explained the logic of referring to port and starboard as opposed to saying left or right when people might be facing different directions. He has a way of explaining things in a direct and respectful way that doesn't feel like a lecture. In between discussions of sailing he showed me how to juggle three balls by standing in front of a wall to ensure that everything I threw was on the correct plane.

This morning he left me with a very old copy of Rilke's *Letters to a Young Poet* while he went to work. The covers are torn off and some pages are missing. I lingered on this passage: "But in every sickness there are many days when the doctor can do nothing but wait. And that is what you, insofar as you are your own doctor, must now do, more than anything else."

And this: "Perhaps all the dragons in our lives are princesses who are only waiting to see us act, just once, with beauty and courage. Perhaps everything that frightens us is, in its deepest essence, something helpless that wants our love."

Learning to sail is an exercise in patience and humility; our fate is dictated by the winds and the water and yet we're able to take some fundamental control over that fate and make micro-adjustments

that get us where we want to go. Sometimes even across an entire ocean.

Getting there requires investing in skills and knowledge that are older than our grandfathers. When we're feeling ungrounded or rudderless, there's no better time to look for the arcs that extend beyond our own lifetimes—long smooth arcs like the fiberglass keel of a sailboat. Submit to the great unspoken grace of the enduring world. At least, that's my hope.

We take the boat out on the calmest day of the year. It is one of those overcast days on the northern coast where sky and sea are the same color gray, and once you get out on the open water you can't see the land anymore and you feel like you're in a Homeric poem where someone has cast a spell to put you in an in-between world. I feel okay for about five minutes and then I start to get seasick. I have a few seconds to plan where I am going to throw up. I try to lean over the railing, but don't get all the way. My half-digested eggs and toast sit on the side of the railing for a few seconds before a wave comes and takes them away. After a year of intense emotional churning, it is satisfying to have my insides come out, to just study them and say, *Well there you are, the roots of all this suffering.* But my sickness doesn't go away after throwing up, or even when we get back to land. I've only been able to help Daniel out with a few lines, tie a few knots—mostly I have been ballast. For this day, his training hasn't paid off. I can't even handle the calmest day of the year on the Pacific. I was upended by something I couldn't see.

The rest of the world keeps insisting that invisible things don't matter, but, like the kite outside the window, just because my frame of reference doesn't show me anything doesn't mean that nothing is there.

# *Two*

SINCE I WAS SIXTEEN I have been on an orbit with music at the center. My traveling companion has been a Blueridge dreadnought acoustic guitar that I bought for three hundred dollars in 1994 at the Fifth String music store in Sacramento.

Dozens of times, I've checked that guitar at the airport, stowing it below the aircraft without worrying about it. I've probably written thousands of songs on it, played hundreds of gigs, and gotten far more than three hundred dollars of use out of it, so I figure if one day I lose it, I'll survive. Yet every time it comes out of the oversized baggage slot next to the golf clubs and surfboards and I see that it hasn't been broken in half, I feel a little like Calvin when he takes Hobbes out of the dryer.

From the instant Nirvana's "Smells Like Teen Spirit" tore out of the speakers on my high school's quad during lunch, I knew I had to find a way to hold something as visceral as that song in my hands. It wasn't a new song anymore, but it was new for me—I had been sheltered from most popular music as a kid. And so my older brother Matt gave me the phone number of his old guitar teacher. At my first lesson I learned how to make a power chord. Days later, Kurt Cobain killed himself. At my next lesson, I pulled out the piece of paper with the chords to "Smells Like Teen Spirit."

"So ... yeah," my teacher said. "That was a bummer. Well, let's hear you play the song."

I only bought his biography after he died. *Here's someone who knows what it means to be sad*, I thought. It sounded noble. Now I just think of him as someone who couldn't stop falling down and hurting himself. Still, I had never thought of lyrics as poetry until I heard him expressing all his confusing contradictions that came closer to the truth by plotting out opposite points.

When I was sixteen, I got myself a subscription to the Time-Life Books series *Voyage Through The Universe.* Every month a cardboard box would arrive containing a new volume showing photos taken from the probes surveying the planets. I remember this little diagram that demonstrated that orbiting is the same as falling, but falling at the same rate that the ground below you falls so that you never crash into the object that you are orbiting.

Earth matches its orbit with Mars three times for every four times it matches up with Venus. In music this is the definition of a triplet, three beats existing in the rhythmic space of four. When you start accenting these notes you get swing music. When you cut out the middle note you get shuffle time. Those simple rhythms are what got people dancing in the twentieth century.

My music was forever changed when I moved to New Orleans at the age of twenty-one. I found a job as a bus boy at the Napoleon House in the French Quarter where they serve a Pimm's Cup topped by a slice of cucumber. When they ran out of cucumbers they'd send me to the A&P to get more, and I would walk across Jackson Square and see the ad hoc jazz band that was assembled on the bench. An invisible benefit to the evolution of music in New Orleans is the thickness of every molecule in the atmosphere there. A trumpet is just a big plunger that moves air, and if that air is thicker it makes a richer sound. Perhaps that's one of the reasons why jazz wasn't invented in a city like Denver.

While living in New Orleans, I wrote a song on my Blueridge called "Bottles on the Tracks" in which I made up a story about a derailed train that was blamed on a man who liked to put empty beer bottles on the tracks so he could hear the smash and the clickety-clack.

> You say that pain is
> something in your heart that you can't fix
> I know what you mean
> I've felt that way since I was sixteen

My dad has always stressed the importance of taking care of one's belongings in order to maintain their resale value. After bashing out chords on it enough times in bars and on street corners, I decided I was never going to sell my guitar and so the resale value wasn't as important as making it mine. I sanded the top down and started to stain it purple. I let the stain dry and sanded it down some more. Somehow the half-purple shade worked and I left it that way. Everyone thought that this discoloration came from sweat or blood and that was fine too.

One night someone left a sticker in my bike basket that said, "I (Heart) New Orleans," one of those cheap ones with the white background and the big red heart. Since I'd already given up on ever selling my guitar, I felt like it was okay to put that sticker on it. Being rough can be a pure expression of love, like when a mother cat grabs her kittens with her teeth and chucks them around. That's how my guitar looked for years, with the half-purple stain and the New Orleans sticker.

In New Orleans, there's an echo of Mars and Venus, and the musicians there take that rhythm and play it as casually as feeding a dog. They are so skillful, but they play like they just don't care, which makes it all so much more compelling.

On September 5, 1977, the day before I was born, NASA launched the Voyager I spacecraft to survey the outer planets. It had a golden record on it with several songs from Earth, a mixtape in case an extraterrestrial came across it. If it were sent today we would probably put a hard drive in there containing MP3s of pretty much everything ever recorded, but there's only so much room on a record. So this mix included Bach's Brandenburg Concerto, some gamelan music from Indonesia, and "Dark Was the Night, Cold Was the Ground," recorded by Blind Willie Johnson, who spent his last days so poor that he slept in a burned-down house.

While Voyager 1 has left our solar system, I've mostly just sat here and thought about stuff. It reached Saturn around the time I was forming the ability to create memories. By 1990 Voyager 1 was able to take a family portrait of all the planets of the solar system, gathered as they were on the black leather couch of space, resembling tiny pixels in a vast darkness. On one of those specks of light, I was cataloging baseball statistics on a PC. I'd invented a simulated baseball game using dice, compiling rosters from the box scores in the newspapers. I would roll the dice for each play, then tabulate the statistics and write a story about each game. Once enough games had been played, I would print out my own newspaper complete with recaps and the accompanying box scores. I'd flesh out the statistics with invented drama and absurdist quotes from the players. "Cubs Manager Don Zimmer was ejected from the game in the seventh inning after arguing with the umpire that, if time is an illusion, we can't be held accountable for our past actions. Said first baseman Mark Grace, 'I guess he was wrong.'"

That computer I typed on was already more powerful than the one that sent the Voyager into space, and now my phone is at least two million times faster at processing data than the car-sized object nineteen billion kilometers away that NASA is trying to communicate with. It's as if we launched the first Pong arcade game into space decades ago and forever after are forced to hack our way into that game to get the answers to our place in the universe.

Dear __________,

Do you know about quantum entanglement? It's when two particles interact in such a special way that even if you separate them, their movements will continue to affect one another. You could be in Los Angeles with one of these particles and I could be in New York, and if your particle spins a certain way, my particle will spin that way, too. This connection happens instantaneously, which is to say that it's faster than the speed of light.

This is such a remarkable scientific fact that I can't understand why everyone isn't talking about it every day. This is more important than health care or algebra or the housing market. You could say that our desire to bridge distance is what is killing us. More and more, we want to get to places faster and we are burning ourselves up to make that happen. It doesn't make any sense. If we are already connected to everything, we can stay right where we are.

There are cords around your heart connecting you to different emotions and places and people. You can't see them physically, but that doesn't matter. When you love something, your heart ties itself around it, like it's tying a string around something it doesn't want to forget. There is a cord that runs from my heart to yours, for example, and it goes right through the center of the earth. It is a long, stretchy cord. Sometimes it has slack in it and I can't feel your pull and I wonder if you're still there, or if you've slipped out of it somehow. Other times it tightens and I can feel every movement and I know what you're feeling without you even telling me. This cord doesn't obey borders or pacts of marriage or care how many babies you've passed through your body. It is an interloper and it breaks all the rules of human society, and maybe that's why nobody wants to talk about it. We don't ever have to talk about it, but still, I promise you, that cord is there.

You don't even have to wait for the achingly slow currents of light to bring you these messages. They are already there.

Yours, presently,
Nick

# *Three*

A COUPLE WEEKS after getting seasick, I find myself with the unique opportunity, at least for a songwriter, to speak at a literary festival in Portland. I'm on a panel with the author Nicholson Baker. He is exactly how you want your authors to be, full of insight and fascinating asides about William James.

Afterwards, I invite him to have coffee with me and my friend Laura. The three of us sit outside the convention center on a concrete ridge while he squints at us in the sunlight. He's interested in our lives as musicians even though Laura and I are both trying to be writers.

"I played the bassoon as a young man," he says. "And I thought I would join the symphony and that would be my life. But I wasn't good enough."

"Do you still play?" I ask.

"No, I haven't touched it in decades," he says.

I find it a little baffling, that you could play an instrument your entire life, then one day sell it and never play it again, but I suppose not very many rock bands are looking for bassoonists.

Yet there is this desire for preservation that runs through all his work. "I've always had an urge to try to hold on to places and documents and buildings," he told *The Paris Review* in 2011. "If a store went out of business when I was a kid, I'd have a horrified, grieving feeling. How could it be gone? What was the shopkeeper going to do now? I don't like when precious things slip through people's fingers—especially things that seem defenseless or under-celebrated, like old newspapers, but also unheralded people who may have said sensible things at a certain time in history, but who were completely drowned out by other people. Or minor poets whose lives were instructive. Sometimes I'm astounded by the absence of sentimentality in other people. How can you not become attached to the poignant scraps that flow through life? I tried to put the date on all my kids' drawings, thinking, *That'll help*. But of course you're trying to save something that's evolving. It isn't savable."

After we finish our coffee, I give Nicholson directions on how to take the streetcar to get to his next function. I walk alone to my car, which isn't actually my car, but my friend Joe's that I've borrowed for a few days while he uses my van to coordinate a film project. As I pull around the corner, I see Nicholson exactly where I left him, waiting for the streetcar. I honk my horn and he turns my way, doing that "Who? Me?" thing, pointing at his chest while I nod vigorously. He grabs his briefcase, runs through the traffic, and joins me in the car. "Thank you," he says. "I guess I could've ended up waiting there a while." After dropping him off at the Jupiter Hotel, I sit there for a moment, just idling, looking at the lingering Portland daylight. Deep in October you get the feeling that any sunny day could be the last for a long while.

Tonight there is a screening in Tacoma of a film I did the soundtrack for. Last night I played a similar screening in Central Washington, driving back this morning for the literary festival. I think about Nicholson and his time with the bassoon. Maybe he appreciated the instrument so much that he was willing to let it go when he realized he wasn't a world-class bassoonist. "Fuck it," I mutter, and get on the highway and drive to Tacoma. The turnout is small and I end up playing just two unamplified songs to about fifteen people. I find myself thinking, more than ever, *These songs are old. I don't believe in them, or this kind of music. But I'm chained to it and I can't let it go.*

I close with "Cincinnati," whose last line is one of endless pining:

> All I want is to be with you
> in a hotel room in Cincinnati
> God that sounds so crude

While I'm putting my guitar back in the case, the people start filing out of the theater. Rick, the director, is giving me this look like, "Get out there!" and I just give him a shrug. The aisle is too narrow for me to squeeze past them so I can open up my suitcase of CDs in the lobby. By the time I get out there, almost everyone has left and I only sell a few. As I pack up and get in my car, Rick shouts from across the street, "Nick, you are a great songwriter, but you are a *terrible* businessman."

Those words keep me awake as I drive the two hours back to Portland. I woke up at five this morning and won't get home until well after midnight. By the time I pull up in front of my apartment, I've driven nearly five hundred miles, participated in a panel discussion, given a beloved author a ride down the street, and played two songs to a mostly empty theater. All I want to do is bury myself in sleep. I take one look at the two guitars in the back of the car and figure I'll just come out in the morning and get them.

When I finally wake up and go outside, the back window of Joe's car is broken. My amp and my electric guitar are still there, but my Blueridge is gone. Some kid probably looked in and saw my stuff and, in a fit of inspiration, broke the window and grabbed the case. If I'd had my van, no one would have seen the guitars through the tinted windows, but in Joe's little car the guitar was all too visible.

I rub at my face, just staring at the broken window. I've never cried over an object before. And then my phone begins to ring. It's my friend Meghann, who lives in New Orleans. The friend who gave me my last name, the friend I called when I got out of a well in San Juan Bautista, having decided to become a musician. I've known her the exact amount of time that I owned my guitar. She wants to know if I could do her a rather large favor by flying to New Orleans that week and driving a Penske truck of her sister's stuff to Sacramento. In any other circumstances I probably wouldn't even consider it, but in the shock of my loss I find myself saying yes. She buys me a plane ticket right then, and a few days later I'm on a plane to New Orleans. This time I have no guitar to ride above.

# Four

My body and my unconscious mind saw the flood coming even if I chose to ignore it. At the beginning of the year, while improvising music in the studio with some friends, I wrote a song called "I Don't Want to Know."

> If surgery is certain
> I don't want to know
> if your titanic heart caves in
> I don't want to know
> if memory persists
> if snipers hold the cards
> I don't want to know
> I don't want to know

A few weeks after writing that song, I drove through Death Valley with my father. We had just passed Badwater Basin, which is also the lowest point in North America, when we had to slow down because we saw a man lying in the road up ahead. As we got closer we saw that the man was holding a camera and taking pictures of a coyote just off the road. We slowed to a stop and looked out the window. The coyote was skinny and haggard and looked me right in the eyes. I thought, *I made eye contact with a coyote. Now I am a coyote.* All we had in the car were homemade brownies from my mom and some leftover lemon peel chicken from the Chinese restaurant the night before, nothing that a coyote should be eating. We kept staring at each other. That brief connection at the bottom of the world felt like it lasted for years. I saw the desperation in its eyes.

I had fallen in impossible love again and the target of my desire told me on a long-distance phone call that what was never really happening was now over. I lay on my couch feeling like I had a cinder block on my chest. I felt I had been the victim of a string of tragedies I couldn't connect. I Googled "plural for crisis" because neither "crisises" nor "crises" sounded right. I left that page open in a tab on my computer, and when I came back to it I was intrigued by the phrase "plural for crisis." What was that? A book? An album? Oh, right. It was my own inability to learn from mistakes.

A month later an energy worker named Tatiana waved her hands and whispered, tearing dark energy from me and shaking it into a bowl of water on the floor. She got the pain moving in me again. It was almost like she was working on a sprained ankle. Afterwards, I was able to feel emotions again, but most of what I felt was a crushing sadness. I would be talking to someone and find that my hand had crept under my jacket to clutch my heart, as if to keep it from gushing blood everywhere. I'd go out to dinner with a nice girl, kiss her goodnight, get in my car, and melt into tears.

Tatiana told me that love was like a beam of light from a star. The star itself might die but we would still see it going on forever in every direction. I had always thought that love was more like a piece of newspaper on fire, which I'd have to keep transferring to other newspapers before it burned out.

I was walking around like a child with a broken truck, showing it to everyone with a sad expectant face hoping someone would fix it for me. But the broken truck was my own heart, and I was just beginning to realize that it had been me more than anyone else who had broken it over and over.

I went to a therapist named Mark whose discipline was Core Energetics, which attempts to solve the issues of the mind by finding their manifestations in the body. I described the pain I felt as a stinging in my stomach. It made me think of someone cruelly poking a sea anemone in a tide pool. Mark asked if I'd ever felt this feeling before. I remembered a family trip to Lake Tahoe when I was seven. Another family with kids my age joined us. It was a sunny day, but I was afraid to play outside and so I pretended I had a stomachache so I could just be alone. Mark asked me if I hated this seven-year-old version of myself. I said, "Of course not," but all my actions in the intervening years had indicated unconscious contempt for him.

One day Mark asked me if I knew about the coyote. At first I thought he was putting me on, like he'd gone through my phone and seen the photo I took in Death Valley. Eventually I realized he was talking about the mythical coyote, the trickster on the edge of the campfire. "Coax him into the light," Mark told me, "so he can't lure you into the darkness anymore."

I told him that I was thinking about signing up for a ten-day meditation retreat, but that I probably wouldn't because it seemed too self-indulgent. He told me that resistance was just my ego's fear of dying, and encouraged me to go through with it.

My friend Mike asked me to play a song at his show at a piano repair shop, where the stage was built on top of several pianos. Just to get on stage, you had to step on the keys and make a horrible sound. I spent the day writing a song on piano just for the show, a song about how everything I did seemed to defeat myself.

> Oh hell
> I know I shoot myself in the foot every day
> I guess at least I never put my foot in my mouth
> because then I'd shoot my mouth off

Our world is built on miracles and yet all around us people are suffering. We see images of war-torn refugees and can identify that as suffering, but we are afraid to acknowledge the suffering in our own lives. We shouldn't be suffering. Our country is not in a civil war and we have food to eat. Maybe some people are better at dealing with that suffering or maybe they're just better at ignoring it. All I know is that I have to do something before I do something much worse.

# *Five*

IF INDEED I have failed at life, I conclude, I might as well check myself into a place that feels like a drug or alcohol rehab center. All the normal methods of being okay with myself aren't working—even a spontaneous trip across the country—and so it has come to this: a Vipassana meditation center in Onalaska, Washington.

The drug I'm addicted to is impossible love, scratched out in dozens of unsent love letters. The thing about impossible love is that even when you are physically alone you have the comfort of your own delusional beliefs. Those give a shape to the world, but when you start to let go of those delusions, everything feels empty and inert, like Frankenstein's monster without the lightning.

When we check in, they divide us into groups of men and women, making it feel a little like prison. On top of that, I have to turn my phone and laptop in at the front desk. From this point onwards, I won't be allowed to talk, read a book, write anything down, use any technology, or do anything to distract myself from the task of learning Vipassana meditation, a very old and arduous technique that requires complete attention to the smallest sensations occurring in your body. They say the proper way to learn it is to devote ten days of your life to it.

The majority of my fellow students are older than I am. Since all we are going to do is meditate, eat, and sleep, and we'll have no contact with the opposite sex, it's already clear that most of the men are going to stay in pajamas the whole day. Living in Portland already feels like wearing pajamas all the time to me, so I've decided to wear chinos, which I quickly discover have a tendency to make my legs fall asleep during meditation.

A few bold deer hang around the campus, probably because the people are so quiet and unthreatening. My first morning, I find myself just a few feet away from one of them, reveling in the gentle grace of the natural world, feeling like I'm becoming closer in temperament to these wild animals by learning to meditate, when the deer bends its knees and lets out a loud gush of piss.

We gather for group meditations three times a day in the big hall. We are each assigned our own cushion on the floor where we can assemble blankets and foam blocks into whatever arrangement makes us comfortable. At every session I experiment, building up a padded throne throughout the day, then tearing it down. We're listening to the recorded voice of a man named Goenka, a former Burmese businessman who in the 1950s had been stricken by migraines. No doctor could help him, but he stumbled on a colony of monks who had kept a meditation technique alive for centuries. After a ten-day session with the monks, Goenka's pain went away. They told him he had learned a technique developed by the Buddha himself 2,500 years ago. Goenka quit his job and devoted himself to spreading this lost practice—first to the people of India, and then to the world—and that's how Vipassana meditation came to Onalaska, Washington.

The meditation itself is simple but not easy. I can see why it fell out of favor with people for two millennia. The first three days of the course we're supposed to observe the sensation of our breath as it comes out of our nostrils. Three times a day, a hundred of us gather in the hall and breathe. Then we head back to our rooms to practice breathing on our own. We wake up at four in the morning and go to sleep at nine—those of us who are able to sleep.

Each moment, on its own, is not unpleasant, especially compared to moments in my life that have been stressful or painful. I'm just sitting here on a pillow, focusing on my nose, but my brain, that ceaseless machine, won't let it be that simple. I think about time all the time, about how far into the hour I am, about how twenty-four hours from now I'll be in the exact same position again, thinking the exact same thoughts. Without access to any of the normal ways of numbing my brain—computers, music, food—I'm just left with my own thoughts spinning around.

My parents left the subject of religion undiscussed when I was growing up. It was just never mentioned. You would think that the binding spiritual practices of the human race would come up at least once in eighteen years, but no. As an adult I appreciate how that gave me no biases against religion. It encouraged me to come to my own conclusions. I used to think that when I died I would still be aware of everything, but that I would have to get in a coffin underground and lie there in the darkness forever, and I wouldn't be able to leave and I wouldn't ever see my family again. This was a terrifying thought and it was reinforced by the *Alfred Hitchcock Presents* episode where a woman tries to escape from prison by befriending the gravedigger of the prison cemetery, who agrees to put her in the coffin with the next prisoner who dies, and dig her up in secret. But then the gravedigger himself dies, leaving her buried alive with his body, and her screams at the realization that no one is going to save her go unanswered. So I had *that* to think about as I was trying to sleep, and that thought kept me awake at night, crying big fat tears until I could calm myself down by thinking that at least I had a little more time before the end. After all, my mother was older than I was and she was still young and laughed at dinner parties.

Here on my padded throne, trying to calm down, I find myself wondering if there's any music I've heard enough times that I have every word and every note memorized. Immediately I think of Paul Simon's *Graceland.* I realize I can just press play in my mind and hear the music roll out, and so I do, starting with the tumbling accordion and the big bright drums of "Boy in the Bubble." I've always wondered why the person he's singing to in that song is crying. He's saying that life is better now, that all our troubles are taken care of. So why would someone be sad?

The first time I heard *Graceland,* my friend Keith was running for seventh grade class president. We sat in his backyard by the pool, painting campaign signs on butcher paper, listening to his boombox. The simple aspects of the music caught my ear: the playful lyrics and horns of "You Can Call Me Al," the bizarre shrieking female background vocals on "I Know What I Know" and the way that same song ends with a rubbery tremolo bassline that sounds like a big fat man buzzing his lips. This was pop music in the best sense of the term; it was accessible and easy to understand while also drawing the listener into a deeper world.

A year later, Keith's brother crashed into a brick wall and died. Just like that. I went to the wake and looked at his body in the casket. His skin was such an odd color and he was dressed so nicely in a suit that I couldn't help but wonder, *Why do people do this to dead bodies?* It certainly helped to reinforce my suspicion that he was still inside his body, sleeping. His body must have still had some sort of life in it, otherwise why would they treat it so well? At the wake I held his mother's hand. She told me that I shouldn't be afraid to come over to the house and play because it would be best if everything went on as normal. She kept squeezing my hand, and I promised I would.

I don't know exactly why, but I never did go over to their house to play again.

For the most part I was a happy kid, and into my teens I was content to play board games with my parents on Friday nights. Then one day in Mr. Gribskov's chemistry class I was sitting next to a pretty red-haired girl named Alice. "What do we know, and what are we looking for?" Mr. Gribskov asked the class every time we started a new problem. This time around, I pretended that I didn't understand the problem so I could go to Alice's house for study group and try to make her laugh, and that was the end of the peaceful naïve happiness. A problem only becomes a problem when you don't know the answer to either one of Mr. Gribskov's questions.

We were learning about how certain atoms are unstable until they pick up the right amount of electrons. Alice was one of triplets, and when I went to her house I entered a world full of stuff I had never considered. She and her sisters baked their own bread, they burned incense, and they listened to records. Vinyl records, by bands like the Velvet Underground, music that I had never heard before.

The world opened up to me, and unfortunately an open world looks a lot like an endless void. I had thought that the world existed on tracks that were already laid down. You bought your bread in a store and it tasted the same every time. Now I had seen that there was no limit to what bread could taste like, but this meant I was facing actual choices for the first time in my life, which meant that there were wrong choices. That's when I first started feeling depressed. I read about Taoism and started listening to Pink Floyd. The I Ching has sixty-four iterations, so I painted a chessboard with one hexagram for every square on the board. Even as I got sadder I always thought that more thinking would untie the knot, that after I had solved a few more equations I could get out of the twisted corridors and find myself in a wide-open meadow of happiness again.

Dear __________,

There is a riveting moment right before an orchestra begins to play when there are a few dozen well-dressed, talented musicians waiting in silence for a man to tell them to start. In that moment they are doing nothing, sitting with their instruments in front of two thousand people in a large concert hall. The silence in that moment is very expensive, very educated. It is of a different quality than you would find in a meadow at dusk.

There is also the moment when a stripper has finished her routine. The music has stopped playing, the energy in the room dissipates, and she puts her clothes back on. I find the way she puts her clothes on to be so much more compelling than the way she takes them off. There is no show in it.

I'd also like to direct your attention to the moment when the first side of a record has finished playing and the needle spills into the center groove and keeps spinning until you get up and turn the record over. The amount of time it takes to get from the last song on the first side to the first song on the other side will always be different. If you're on top of it, it might just be a few seconds. However, if you're otherwise occupied—if there's a cat on your lap, if the egg yellows are congealing, if you're getting to second base—it might be a while before the record gets flipped. There is nothing the maker of the record can do to dictate how long this will last.

Waiting,
Nick

# *Six*

When I enrolled in college, I was drawn to archaeology. My professor Ruben was a gentle man who worked to secure the first-ever dig at San Juan Bautista Mission. Even though I was a freshman taking his class with no particular ambitions to be an archaeologist, he gave me the opportunity to dig at the site.

San Juan Bautista Mission was the setting of the last scene of the Alfred Hitchcock film *Vertigo*, in which Jimmy Stewart's obsession with the platinum blonde swirl in Kim Novak's hair finally boils over, and he follows her up a bell tower only to watch her slip over the edge when she's startled by a nun.

It's also where the writers Joan Didion and John Dunne married in 1964. Didion was born in Sacramento and often writes about the burden of mythology on the state of California. I believe in the magic of California and I have the state motto "Eureka" tattooed on my wrist. The word means, "I have found it," in honor of the flood of people who came to the state in the nineteenth century looking for gold. When I was twelve I went on a student exchange trip to Matsuyama, Japan, where I gave a presentation in front of a roomful of people about James Marshall discovering gold at John Sutter's mill on the American River. I knew how to say my name in Japanese: "Watashi wa Nick desu." The rest I said slowly in English as a Japanese man interpreted for everyone. *How do I know he's actually translating what I'm saying?* I wondered.

California has always been a place for those inclined to dig. First it was the Spanish laying down El Camino Real, then the prospectors looking for gold, then it was the Beats in North Beach. Everyone who heads west is stopped by the ocean and must look down. If they don't find anything beneath them, they end up digging into their own minds and end up becoming beach crazy, the condition of certain lost people in coastal towns who can't go back and can't go forward.

"Who digs Los Angeles IS Los Angeles," Allen Ginsberg wrote in *Howl,* and I believe he meant that if you like a place you become a part of that place, and you become a reason for that place to be liked by others. Or maybe he meant that the more you search for yourself, the more you separate yourself from those who aren't searching for anything.

When I arrived at college my new roommate had a poster of the Iron Maiden album *Can I Play With Madness?* hanging on the wall, the one with the skeleton hand digging through a guy's skull to pull out his brains. I hated that image so much, and I had to look at it every day when I got out of bed. It was such a bummer to leave the tranquility of dreamland and have to face that poster. It was probably part of the reason why I dropped out of college.

The school was California State University at Monterey Bay, and in retrospect it was kind of a rip-off. Only recently when I was driving through the campus again and I saw all the buildings that went up after I left did it occur to me that my parents were paying a lot of money for a half-built school. The university was built on the decommissioned Fort Ord Army Base. The year was 1995, and I suspect the whole project was moved ahead to provide a good stop for Bill Clinton's re-election campaign. Six months before school started a tour guide showed us around and said, "This is where the library will be, and this is where the student union will be." She held up a drawing of what it would look like, with happy people sketched in. I imagined myself as one of those happy sketch-people, going to the sketch-library, but when I showed up for the first day of class, the campus looked exactly like it did on the tour and not at all like the sketches. There were still buildings with murals encouraging us to "Shoot First or Die." We slept in barracks. There was no library.

The fat, rubbery leaves of ice plant covered the hills all over campus. A few decades earlier, the plant had been brought over from Africa to stabilize soil erosion on the coastal dunes. It thrived, but ended up contributing to the soil erosion instead of fixing it. Between the seventies and the nineties the state went from propagating the plant to identifying it as an invasive species and pulling it out by the roots. During my environmental studies class they asked us to pull out as much ice plant as we could, as we were cheaper labor than Mexican immigrants.

Before they're introduced, invasive species usually sound like great ideas. In the 1890s, Eugene Schieffelin, chairman of the American Acclimatization Society, decided that every species of bird mentioned in the plays of William Shakespeare should exist in North America. Schieffelin brought over a group of a hundred starlings from England and set them loose in Central Park. There are now more than two hundred million starlings throughout the continent, all because Shakespeare mentioned one in *Henry IV, Part I.* Rarely has an author's pen had such consequences. Imagine if a revised manuscript turned up where Shakespeare crossed out "starling" in favor of "warbler."

We can't get all the starlings back in the bag, of course. In the play a starling is introduced because Hotspur wants to drive Henry mad by having a bird repeat the name of Hotspur's imprisoned brother-in-law Mortimer.

Growing up in Northern California made me a member of the large group of people who don't want to think that they live in Southern California. I've always been curious about where the border between Northern and Southern California is. On tour of California once, I made it a habit to ask everyone where they thought the border would be if California were to actually split in two. Whether I was in San Francisco or Santa Barbara, the answer was the same: "The border would be just south of the city limits." At first I thought that was stupid coming from people living in what was so clearly Southern California. But then I remembered that when I was growing up in Sacramento I imagined that Southern California began just south of my city. None of us want to admit that we live in Southern California. Maybe we all do.

California might mean more to people outside of it than to those who live there. On that trip to Japan, my host father told me he felt a connection to Sacramento because the word "sacrament" was sitting right there in plain view. I had never really thought about the name of my own city, but hearing him say it aloud made me soften towards it. He was the first person to tell me that there are more trees per capita in Sacramento than in any other city in the world except for Paris, a fact that no one ever believes and which I myself doubt once a year and have to look up again to be sure.

As a kid I wondered why the Golden Gate Bridge was orange and not gold until I realized that "golden" referred to the Golden State, and not the color of the bridge. Early in *Vertigo,* right under that bridge, Jimmy Stewart dives into the bay to rescue Kim Novak.

They're at Fort Point, which was built just before the Civil War to prevent enemy ships from attacking. That no ships ever came close doesn't matter as much as knowing that even then, California was ready for the worst.

A few years ago, my friend Chris was in a production of *Macbeth* at Fort Point. Most of the actors lost their voices trying to shout over the winds that are always swirling through the old masonry. Early on in the play a sergeant is asked if an attack on the Scots by the Norwegian king dismayed Macbeth. The sergeant replies that this doesn't trouble Macbeth: "Yes, as sparrows dismay eagles, or the hare the lion." A joke that launched sparrows across the Atlantic.

I'd always thought that college would be the place where I would be able to study what I wanted to study. I couldn't wait to go to a university library and have unlimited access to knowledge. I imagined that I would be one of those students who stayed in college for a decade, not wanting to leave.

According to the career-finder test we took in high school, I should be a technical writer. I've always imagined that a technical writer's job is to sit there with a video player and a screwdriver for as long as it takes to understand how it works. I suspect that all my favorite writers are technical writers, but instead of examining video players they're just sitting there examining themselves, and instead of a screwdriver they have a pen.

So I went to college with the vague idea of being a technical writer. What I really wanted was to sit in the library and read books and explore, but it turned out there was just an empty lot where the library was supposed to be. At least there was an archaeology class.

I imagine if you are really trying to be an archaeologist, there's a bunch of paperwork to get through before you're allowed to dig, but that wasn't my experience. I was digging for artifacts the first week of class. The spoils usually go to the people who care the least.

No amount of uprooting ice plant or sifting for broken pottery could change the fact that I was just another invasive species attracted to the beauty of California. My parents are from the Midwest, and after they got married in Chicago in 1969 my dad was offered an engineering job in Sacramento. They looked the city up in an *Encyclopedia Britannica* and read about the trees and decided it would be a fine place to spend the rest of their lives. This was a lot more research than I did when choosing my college. I thought the name Monterey sounded nice and went towards it.

In my dorm room in the barracks, underneath the Iron Maiden poster, I started recording music on a four-track. I wrote some of my first songs, mostly trying to impress a particular girl. This felt better than covering Beatles songs and putting her name in the lyrics, which is what I had been doing. One day when I was playing around on my guitar I came up with what I thought was a cool riff. I didn't have any words yet, so I headed to the dining hall for dinner. As I was walking I started thinking about that girl, and how she didn't seem to like me the way that I liked her, and that she drank too much and was too erratic. I probably looked like I was losing it, balling up my fists, talking to myself. I was rehearsing the words that I wanted to say to her: "You're sooo ... dramatic," the pause acknowledging my participation in the drama.

I was excited about the possibility of this phrase fitting with the riff I'd been working on. Instead of going to dinner I rushed back to my room and put the two parts together. This was the first time I had created the music and lyrics separately and combined them in such a way that they actually fit. Perhaps that's what magic is: the synthesis of science and art. You build a structure and leave a space for humanity. At that moment I simultaneously knew what

I wanted to do with my life and realized that I was in the wrong place to do it.

Aside from the archaeology class, the school had little to offer. Music isn't something you should be learning in school anyway. It's something you should be thinking about on a Greyhound bus between Knoxville and Wheeling.

And another thing: that goddamn Iron Maiden poster.

Every other weekend I would go up to San Francisco to visit a friend. I couldn't stop thinking about dropping out of school. Her apartment building was on a hill in the Lower Haight, right in front of a church. When I walked towards her building at night all I could see of the church was a big white cross glowing above.

She was trying to convince me to move up to San Francisco. It was an international city, full of excitement, she said, and I could come stay with her for a while.

In *Vertigo*, Jimmy Stewart is investigating a woman who he thinks may be possessed by the soul of her great-grandmother. It turns out that her erratic behavior is just a ploy to trick him, and he becomes the one possessed. I was at the edge of becoming obsessed with songwriting, and he who likes songwriting IS songwriting, as Ginsberg might say.

I was in the middle of writing a song—a constant state, really—and thinking about that church in San Francisco one hot day in archaeology class. Each of us had been assigned our own place to dig. I was waist-deep in an old abandoned well that had long been filled with dirt. After several weeks of looking for stuff, not a single artifact had been uncovered. If you're not finding anything, archaeology is really just shoveling dirt around.

I looked up at the mission from down in the well. The bell tower from *Vertigo* wasn't actually there. It had been a temporary thing for the movie; Hitchcock had looked at the mission and seen a bell tower where there wasn't one.

My pickaxe hit a soft spot and a simple cross made out of white abalone shell popped out of the ground. It was maybe two inches long and still had a shine to it once the dirt was brushed off. When I held it at arm's length it looked exactly like that glowing cross in San Francisco. I was excited to have found something for my professor Ruben, and for the mission, but more than anything, I knew what it meant for me. I grabbed the cross and climbed out of the well, calling everyone over. Ruben was pleased. The padre shook my hand. It would be the first artifact that would go in the mission's new museum.

"I'm not telling you to make the world better," Joan Didion said to the class of 1975 at UC Riverside. "Because I don't think that progress is necessarily part of the package. I'm just telling you to live in it. Not just to endure it, not just to suffer it, not just to pass through it, but to live in it. And if you ask me why you should bother to do that, I could tell you that the grave's a fine and private place, but none I think do there embrace. Nor do they sing there, or write, or argue, or see the tidal bore on the Amazon, or touch their children. And that's what there is to do and get it while you can and good luck at it."

I didn't stick around four years to hear what would be said at my own commencement address. Didion's words were enough. I wiped the dirt from my hands and walked across the street to a pay phone to call Meghann to tell her I was dropping out of college.

# *Seven*

A MAN AND A WOMAN are sitting cross-legged at the front of the meditation hall. They are our teachers, modeling the kind of calmness we're supposed to be feeling.

The person closest to me is a fidgeter. Every thirty seconds, another fidget. In addition to being silent, the goal in meditation is to not move at all. As the week unfolds, we're supposed to be increasingly vigilant about staying still. The fidgeter wears a jacket in every session, one of those light waterproof ones that makes a shooshing every time it moves. Out of one hundred still and quiet people, it's just my luck to be stuck next to the douchebag in a windbreaker.

Whenever I encounter someone I don't like, I try to relax and think about what it will be like a long time from now, after our sun has died out and all the stars in the sky have collapsed and all the matter in the universe reverses course and hurtles toward one infinitesimally small point in a reverse Big Bang. Every particle that has ever existed, every person that you've ever loved or hated, all the city buses, the bottles of hair spray, lost mixtapes, the early notes for the lyrics to the Eagles' "Take It Easy," all of that will squeeze into a container much smaller than the elevator in an old building, and we will all have to learn how to get along and find something to talk about. For one-billionth of a second, that is, until the universe Big Bangs again.

The meditation sessions are designed to focus us on direct experience as opposed to blind ritual. Goenka speaks of going into the cells of our bodies and extracting the suffering. Performing surgery on ourselves, in other words. Up until now, I've never really considered the possibility of changing the fundamental nature of myself. Once cells are set in motion, I've always thought, they will carry that momentum for life.

The brain tells the story of our consciousness, but that story is not the absolute truth. You can stare at your bookcase full of books, wonderful books written by inspiring people, and you can think about how splendid the world is, how much you are loved by your friends, and how everything is going to be all right. Then, with no change in the actual world, your brain can tell you that everything is shit, that all those books are lies, or at least pale attempts to cover up the pointless suffering of the world, that all your friends are just laughing at you, that everything is not going to be all right. All the while that bookshelf sits there. The words never change.

My drum teacher Gavin used to talk about getting into the groove of a song. It's called a groove, he explained, because it's the same thing as a woodworker using a plane to wear a path in a piece of wood. Each pass of the tool makes it easier to find that groove again, and makes it more real. When you make a groove with music you are establishing a place where peoples' bodies can move, where they can attract each other, where they can fall in love and create their own grooves. That's why falling in love cuts so deep: you actually cut a groove into your brain because it feels so good, and you don't realize how deep into the canyon you've gotten until it's too late.

Dear __________,

I saw a picture of conjoined gray whales that had washed up on the beach in Mexico. They were attached at the hip. They had only lived a short while after birth, yet their big mouths looked more like smiles of contentment than anything else I've seen today.

I thought—foolishly, I know—well, *that is us.* Too connected to swim off on our own. Too encumbered by our own ties to survive as individuals.

For every one weird thing we find on a beach in Mexico there are ten stranger things that live and die in the deep black never to be illuminated by flashbulbs. Likewise, for every person who comes up to us with unexpected kindness, there are probably ten more whose path we'll never trip over, who will never clap us on our backs as we raise our mugs at the tavern.

The suggestion of what might still be out there is what keeps us hunting.

I remember hearing as a kid that when a zoo first puts an elephant in captivity, they have to use the strongest chains possible because the elephant constantly tries to escape. But after a few weeks or so they don't need the big chain anymore. They can keep an adult elephant captive with a tiny piece of rope. Just the suggestion of a chain is enough.

Oh, the things they casually tell kids at school. You never know what off-hand anecdotes will wind up in someone's mind thirty years later.

Careful what you say,
Nick

# *Sadness: a field guide*

I DON'T WANT TO SAY that modern life is a jungle, that we have tamed the wild of nature in creating our civilizations and yet allowed the random and the chaotic to remain, that although we might not fear the tiger and the boa in our daily walks we still have great monsters to fear, monsters that we have neither the guns to shoot nor the armor to protect ourselves from.

Nor do I want to imply that I have walked farther, faster, stronger, or that I have seen more. I haven't seen anything. I have felt a smoldering unease in my gut on warm August evenings, and I have danced with a pretty girl once or twice.

However, when arriving in a new city some orientation is welcome to even the most seasoned traveler, and I have been to this city. I know my way around. I offer you some points of interest.

**WISTFULNESS**

This is a tender sadness. Romantic. It is full of an inexpressible feeling of life being better, more real, more fun, some other time, somewhere. Of the old house, where you could dance to music that felt fresh and new. Of the old town, with the easy river access that no one would ever use because there was a new mall just built. It's easy to forget that those times weren't happy while they were occurring. They're only happy now, in retrospect, in relation to the present.

**LETHARGY**

This is a poor excuse for sadness. This is dragging a sack of tuba bells behind you. Where are you taking them? The world is a narrow sidewalk. Look behind you at all the eager people who can't squeeze by, who just want to make it to the end of the block to buy a burrito. These are the prisoners of your lethargy.

**MELANCHOLY**

The Greeks thought that this came from an excess of black bile. Where does the black bile come from? Are you born with it? Do you inhale it somehow? Is it related to diet? Does it start off a different color and then turn black? How much time can you spend thinking about black bile before you start to get sick?

This is perhaps the best type of sadness to achieve. Morrissey sang about it often.

This is a thrilling, romantic, ennobling sadness. This is your body screaming with joy, if joy can be taken out of its normal association with happiness. This is the sadness of a well-lit grocery store full of people you'll never talk to. The sadness of a glimpse of your city from the crest of a hill, the bridges drawn to let a barge through. The sadness from only being allowed to live one life, and having to choose what to do, and not muck it up by spreading yourself too thin. The sadness of not being able to be everywhere at once, to be at every party, audit every course, drive every parkway, taste every dessert. The sadness of loving a song, wanting to live inside a song, wanting to kiss every person you see. The sadness of having a body, of not being able to levitate and glide down the hill. The sadness of walking through a library feeling like you're in a morgue, and wanting to rescue every neglected book, knowing that no matter how many books you read, you'll still never read even one-tenth of one percent of all the books at your local library.

Don't try to shrug off melancholy. It's the kind of sadness that will take you somewhere. It will admit you to certain clubs. Let it happen.

**DESPAIR**

At least it's not permanent. Embedded in its DNA is the knowledge that it is an aberration and that there will soon be a correction, a return to the mean. It is perhaps the only time mathematics can help you get out of a sadness.

**DEPRESSION**

This is serious.

This is the finger of God on your chest, pinning you down. Not the God that children pray to at night, asking for help with passing the next level on their video games. It's the God who hates the naked body. Who hates dancing. The cartoon God who gets cranky when He leans back on a cloud and accidentally sits on a thunderbolt, and who throws that thunderbolt down with not a care in the world whom it might hit.

Depression is being unemployed and being too sad to look for work, too sad to make a phone call when you see a promising advertisement for employment, too sad to even answer the phone when it's probably someone offering work. Depression is having a gun and being too limp to point it at your head, instead letting its weight pull your arm down, down, down. When you are depressed, you are quite literally shooting yourself in the foot.

**MISERY**

This is life in the trenches. This is digging down when you need to look up. This is going to take some train tickets and yard sales to undo. Maybe the time has come to try to lift this tarp off of you. Even if it's just one corner of the tarp, even if lifting it leaves the tarp flapping in the wind. You need to be able to see.

**TORPOR**

This is livened by the dictionary's whimsical suffixing of the word for adjectival use into the word "torporific."

**REGRET**

Time is not a boomerang. Time is not TiVo. Time is not an airport shuttle. Time does not loop around and come back for stragglers. Time does not exchange your ticket if you slept through the boarding call. Time is not a pigeon with a compass in its beak. Time doesn't know where it's going. It doesn't care. Time cuts through canyons and farmlands, through homes and cities. Time takes the easiest route. Regret implies that time has some sort of culpability. Time takes no such responsibility! Time issues no receipts. Time is a barreling locomotive on the loose, sliding down the tracks into what you thought was a station but is really just a phone booth, a drinking fountain, a pile of stones. It's a cardboard cutout of a shelter. It's a soggy spoonful of discount cornflakes.

**GUILT**

This is a self-imposed verdict, handed down by a jury deep inside your heart. There is no punishment, though. There is no penance. So the guilt remains. If only hard labor could work it off. If only solitary confinement could make it right. Perhaps the judgment should come with a sentence. Why not? The jury is all imagined, anyway. You have been sentenced to bake a cobbler, then go to the big bookstore in town where you must buy a daily newspaper from a city you've never been to. Arbitrary, sure, but not any more arbitrary than the punishments they hand out in some courtrooms.

**WOE**

Homophonous with "Whoa." It's a surprising sadness, a sadness that stops you in the middle of your walk. "Whoa. What happened?" Then you sit down and try to retrace your steps. "Whoa. This is really something." You can't even remember how you got to where you are. Who knows if you'll ever get back? "Whoa."

**HEARTACHE**

This is walking on the edge of a sword, staying on that blade even though it hurts, because you know that slipping and falling will be even more painful. This is life behind the gates of a train crossing, waiting and waiting for a train to pass, a train that is too long for you to even count the number of cars. Then the train slows, and stops, and backs up, while you sit there waiting for it to pass.

**SORROW**

You can only attain sorrow if something bad has actually happened to you, which sets it apart from most other types of sadness. Sorrow is something you wear, like a cloak. People can see it on you and they don't ask you to remove it when you come into their homes from the cold. In fact, they're pleased to see someone wearing such a finely tailored garment. They look at their own clothes and realize how cheap they are. Then they turn away, ashamed that they would wish for such a heavy cloak.

**DOLEFULNESS**

Dolefulness makes your eyes big and round, and when your eyes are big and round they can let in more light. At least you haven't stopped seeing.

**EXISTENTIAL SADNESS**

Sadness about the state of being sad. This is an acknowledgment of the futility of thinking about sadness, of writing lists about the different kinds of sadness.

**GRIEF**

This is someone torn away from you, your fingers having curled around their heart and their soul, and then having your fingers ripped off.

**UNHAPPINESS**

This is not sadness. You spend your whole life at a cocktail party, hosted by influential and powerful people. Rich people. Not to say that you are rich or powerful or influential yourself necessarily, but you've been invited to their party. You belong there. You can tell the difference between a torte and a tart just by glancing at a teetering silver tray. You don't enjoy menthols, but you'll accept them if they're all that's offered to you. You can explain how Foucault influenced your gender identity. You even know how to joke about the very subject of gender identity. You laugh at the right moments, along with everyone else. You put your hand on someone else's forearm when you reach the exciting part of the story.

Unhappiness is when you step outside the party for a brief respite. You walk out on the veranda and are momentarily surprised at how dark and cold it has gotten since you arrived at the party. Your arms cross your chest and you hold your shoulders in a tight shiver as you look over the hedges and boulevards. You sense something wrong. Nothing is wrong. You can always return to the party. The door is unlocked.

### DISMAY

This is only for kings and vicars. Common people don't know the shame of prematurely having to abdicate the throne or the disappointment of hearing about the divorce of a man and woman in one's parish, a man and woman who had been counseled on the subject of divorce, who were told to give it a thousand more chances, because God gives you so many chances.

Dismay can only befall you if you own an estate or live in a soap opera. Dismay is when your fortunes have gone south, and your fortunes are oil wells and dairy farms. Dismay is righteous and grand, and bigger and more important than most anything, worthy of headlines just below the fold on the front pages of regional newspapers. However, it lacks the depth of almost any other kind of sadness. It is a minor-league sadness, striving for a spot on the roster.

### HAPPINESS

Don't let the name fool you. This is also sadness.

This is perhaps the most desperate form of sadness there is. Think of all the lists you make, full of reasons why you should be happy, why you are happy, damn it. Apple wedges with cheese. City parks. The volatility of the stock market. The way she hugged you from behind, unexpectedly, at that New Year's Eve party. Aren't those also the reasons why you're sad?

Happiness is running to the post office with a mixtape for a friend, having quickly thrown on a baseball-style shirt with a number on the back because of the heat. But happiness only lasts for a moment. After all, you're running in pleated pants, which look stupid. Any second now, you'll realize that.

# *Eight*

I HAVE BEEN FIRED more times than anyone I've ever met, yet never once has someone said the words "You're fired" to me. Like so many things that happen in the movies, getting fired is less exciting in real life.

I've also never heard someone say the words "You're hired." Getting and losing jobs has always been very nebulous. At the end of an interview someone will say, "Well, can you come in on Monday?" Looking back, I've never been sure if I actually had *any* job. Whenever I hear, "Yeah, we don't need you to come in on Monday," I always have the urge to ask, "Well, how about Tuesday?"

I don't think I've ever been fired because I didn't get the job done. I'm sure it was because of my attitude. I've never done a good job of disguising the fact that when I finish the work they give me, I proceed to do my own work. All these years, I probably would have been much better off if I'd worked harder at *pretending* to work, because the illusion of workers working is what is valued most highly in workplaces.

I love working. Work is just doing stuff, building stuff, making stuff, cleaning stuff. And yet the kind of work I've often found myself getting paid for is so different than the kind of work I love doing. Instead of building toward a career in a secure field, in the name of freedom I've often taken the jobs that mean the least: temporary jobs.

I was hired and fired from Kaiser-Permanente in Portland six times, and each time I'd come back to a different section of the building and work for a different supervisor. One time I was working on the sixth floor and I was lucky enough to have my own cubicle. One of my responsibilities involved making copies of a particular form and then putting each of those photocopied forms back in the copier and copying something on the other side of the paper. However, as soon as the ink is affixed by a copy machine, the paper has undergone a fundamental change. This is why the page is warm and shiny when you pull it out. The machine doesn't like it when you put that same piece of paper through it again.

Eventually the machine stopped working. I told my supervisor and she gave me the number of the copy machine repairman. It's strange to think how often, when I'm new on the job, I've ended up with a responsibility I probably shouldn't have. I called the repairman and he met me back at the copy machine. After he fixed it, he told me that I couldn't just put the same piece of paper back in the machine because the machine would keep breaking. I explained that the only way I could do my job was to put the paper through the copy machine two times, and he told me that the copy machine would keep breaking if I did that and he'd have to keep coming back to fix it. I told him that I didn't know how else to do what they were asking me to do, except to put it through twice. It was his job, he said, to fix copy machines, and he didn't care if it was the same machine over and over again.

I began to wonder how many other people were spending their days in situations like these. How many people were doing something so disconnected from what they really cared about that their primary goal was to make it through the day without conflict?

In most jobs you can look around and find the one person who really knows what's going on. Often this is not the boss, it's just the person who actually cares about the work getting done. In every office there is a dance of uncaring people around this one overcaring person. The point of the dance is to run out the clock: to walk slowly to and from the bathroom, to stare at a piece of paper, to put files into boxes and take them back out, while the overcaring person harrumphs and fills out his or her daily reports. It's as if you asked a group of improvisers to act like they were working in an office. It's almost funny to watch. And then it's not.

I had another job where I worked in a warehouse near the airport. Because we were working with electronics, we had to be protected from static electricity, so there was a big blue rubber mat on my desk and I wore a strap around my wrist, which plugged into a grounding device. I understood its purpose, but it was hard not to feel like I was connected to a machine that was monitoring all my actions. I tried not to dwell on the *Matrix* implications. Eventually I learned to ignore the strap, which meant that sometimes when I needed to go to the bathroom I would be yanked back into my chair.

The first day at that job, about an hour in, the guy sitting in front of me turned around and started talking to the guy sitting behind me.

"So I'm in this warehouse last night, right? And it's really dark, so I light a flare. And right when I do that I see this guy in front of me with a knife. I try to pull up my shotgun, but he's too close, so I hit him in the face with the barrel, and he falls backward off the balcony. Then his buddy comes up behind him and I blow a hole right through his chest. It was awesome."

I was frozen for the first half of his narrative, but then decided that he was talking about a video game. He had to be, right? I couldn't picture this guy with glasses and a ponytail actually hitting someone with a shotgun barrel.

Halfway through my first day, the boss called a meeting so he could tell us about how the company was really hurting that month. The problem, he explained, was that they weren't moving enough high-revenue items. I hadn't yet figured out how the company made money, so I wasn't shocked to find that they weren't making enough. The boss said that they'd tried to think of everything they could, and the only solution was to cut everyone's hours back to thirty a week. He gave us a fearful smile and said that it was just short-term and not personal. He finished by asking if anyone had any suggestions, anything at all, for how the company could make more money. He gave us a minute to think it over, or pretend to think it over, in complete silence. I had no idea what that company did or how it could possibly have any money to hire people in the first place, so I just kept quiet.

There are two types of temp jobs. One situation is an office that has been overwhelmed with work and has been forced into seeking outside help. As a temp worker, this is the situation you want. Everyone is glad to see you, because every little thing you do is a bonus. There wasn't anyone there before you to do this work, and now, magically, you are here taking care of it, as if a little elf has arrived to make everything easier.

The other kind of situation is when you're replacing someone who's out due to sickness or vacation. This is going to be a terrible experience. This is the "You're not Elizabeth," assignment, because everyone in the office who sees you for the first time is expecting to see Elizabeth and get some help from her because she knows how to do this certain thing, but instead they see you, dumb old you, and even though you're a guy, or especially because you're a guy and they're trying to temper their disappointment with humor, they say, "*You're* not Elizabeth." Which you're supposed to laugh at, because all office humor, whether it's "I hate Mondays," or "Thank God it's Friday," has the subtext of, "Please fucking kill me." I have a feeling that even more than my distaste for pretending to work, not finding the "You're not Elizabeth" joke funny is what got me fired. To me, laughing at that joke would have felt like holding out my hands for the handcuffs. I wanted to laugh with joy instead of pain.

I watched the film *Office Space* one night after work and it was almost too much to take. There's a character named Michael Bolton who always has to deal with people telling him that he has the same name as a famous singer, as though he didn't know that already. The day after I saw that movie I was in my little cubicle with a list of names I was supposed to cold call. Next to me was a woman with a list of her own. We all hated cold calling, and did everything we could do avoid being left with those names. It was like we'd been asked to slaughter lambs, but at least on a farm we'd have ended up with lamb chops for dinner. I was staring at my list of names, trying to figure out how I could get through them all or get out of calling them when my cubicle neighbor turned to me with a look of pure joy and said, "Oh my God! There's someone on here named Michael Bolton! Like the singer!"

Had she seen the movie? Did she know that I had *just* seen the movie? My expressionless face probably terrified her, and she turned back to her phone. Later that day the boss told me he didn't need me to come in on Monday.

Just because I kept digging my own grave didn't mean I wasn't suffering. I never wanted to be fired. On the long walks home, I'd rehearse what I'd say to my wife Amanda. I dreaded trying to explain why I'd lost another job. "I guess they ran out of work for me," I'd say. "I don't know what happened."

I worked in another warehouse near the airport that boxed up cellphones to ship out to customers. The conveyor belt would roll them past and I'd have to install the battery and send them along. It was frustrating to know that these phones were heading out to every corner of the country. These phones were living the life I wanted to live: traveling, connecting, communicating.

The week the Internet bubble burst, I was working in the Trump Building on Wall Street. The NASDAQ peaked on Friday, March 10th, 2000. My first day was the following Monday. I worked on the eleventh floor at an investment capital company. I was in the corner of a big room where a bunch of guys were calling potential investors and trying to soothe their collective anxiety. They kept telling these people that the market was really volatile at the moment, but that they needed to ride it out. They kept saying that word, volatile, all week. I bet someone came in and coached everyone on how to use the word volatile. You could see everything you needed to see about these men by how much they hunched over their phones. If they leaned back in their chairs and let their stomachs stick out, they were protected from all the chaos, or at least believed themselves to be. If they were curled up over their phones pressing their temples they had no contacts left to call.

These men were little specks on in the ocean of the stock market, and their job was to act like they had some ability to navigate those volatile seas. It was incredible to be there at the top, in the building named after the most famous American moneyman, on the street synonymous with greed, just after the technology stock market hit its highest point in history. You would think that it would be glorious to be at the top, but all I saw was terror.

One time in Portland I was called in to replace an Elizabeth at the reception desk of a medical center. The reception desk is a horrible place to land, because everything that happens there depends upon personal connections and idiosyncratic knowledge of that particular office. It doesn't matter how good you are at typing or taking messages, you're constantly disappointing everyone. "*You're* not Elizabeth." "I'm sorry I'm not Elizabeth, but can I help you with something?" "I'll just wait until Elizabeth comes back." If I could have somehow imbibed all of Elizabeth's spirit, if the temp agency would have allowed me to put a straw in Elizabeth's brain and drink up her knowledge, I would have done that.

This particular Elizabeth, I learned, was out of the office because her mom had died. Whenever you get a temporary assignment, you're always trying to gauge how long it will last. It feels heartless to react to a death so coldly, but what's the difference between you and Sam Spade investigating the murder of Miles Archer? You're both just looking for clues. In this case, it seemed to me that an Elizabeth grieving for her mother would be out for a while. Indeed, the agency told me it'd probably be a week. Even though the first day was rough, I still needed the job, and enough people were starting to accept that I wasn't Elizabeth. I came in the next morning wanting to do my best.

I was surprised to walk into the reception area to see Elizabeth herself sitting at the desk, answering phone calls. Her eyes didn't look puffy or tear-stained. She was handling all the calls and packages that I had stumbled over the day before. It looked effortless. It was the only time in all my temping when I ever came face-to-face with an actual Elizabeth, the mythical creature that I was always replacing. She was such a professional Elizabeth that even the death of her own mother, the ur-Elizabeth, didn't waylay her for more than a day. My heart broke for her. I wouldn't want to do anything for weeks after the death of someone I cared so much about, but now I wonder if maybe this was her choice. Maybe it was her way of working through the grief, to be in a place where she was useful, where she played a role that people appreciated. After all, that is the most important thing that work can give you, a place where you can belong and contribute. When I saw Elizabeth, I turned around and went home, happy to have a day off.

# *Nine*

THE FIRST PERSON to circumnavigate the world was a slave. His name was Enriqué. He was captured by Ferdinand Magellan on one of the explorer's early trips to Malaysia. Magellan brought his new slave back to Spain with him, then brought him along on his trip around the world, one that Magellan himself did not survive. Because Enriqué had come from Malaysia to Spain, he had already traveled further than the rest of the crew, so when they reached Asia again, Enriqué was completing the first-ever circumnavigation. Because he was a slave almost nothing is known about him. Magellan gets credit for being the first around the world, even though he himself never made it all the way.

So let's not underestimate what can be accomplished even when you have no freedom.

When I finally visited a prison—an actual prison, with concrete walls and razor-wire fences—I started to think about how much freedom I actually have. The quest to become successful at music seems almost inseparable at times from the quest to become famous. To be a prisoner is the opposite of being famous. No one sees you, no one writes about you, no one knows your name. You are as close to not existing as a person can be, and when you actually do stop existing it's possible that no one will remember you. Maybe the worst part of prison is that you don't get to be in the world any more. Not just that you're not allowed to see the world, but that you're not allowed to be seen by the world. You've lost the privilege to be known.

I was booked to play four shows at Folsom Prison with my band, which included Danah, a cellist, and Dorota, a violinist. I'd only recently met the two of them. We were joined by my longtime trumpeter, John. Our first rehearsal was in Marshall Park in downtown Sacramento on a Sunday night. It was the same night my friend Stelth played on the Grammy Awards in Los Angeles with The Lumineers, who were nominated for Best New Artist.

Usually when I play a show, there is some part of me that hopes that more will come of a particular performance than just what happens in that room: maybe someone important will see me play and want to help my career, maybe lots of people will tweet about it, or photos and recordings will get passed around. Maybe I'll meet a girl and fall in love. However, there is no Internet in prison. There is no one to fall in love with. There are no cellphones. There are no important members of the music industry. No one will hear about what happens in that room.

We met our consigliere Jim at the gates and he helped guide us through the different checkpoints that bring visitors further inside the prison. The women had been told to dress modestly and not reveal any skin. We had to measure Danah's skirt to make sure it was the appropriate length. I asked Dorota what it felt like to be able to incite riots based on how she dressed. She said half-jokingly that it felt "powerful."

When that heavy lock clanked free and the door opened up to lead us out of the dark vestibule into the bright Folsom Prison yard, my left knee wobbled. Check-in had been so slow and unexciting that when we finally saw daylight we couldn't help but be struck with the realization, *Oh, this is it.* These were now actual prisoners walking around. Some of them had probably killed people or, you know, worse.

But instead of *The Shawshank Redemption*, I was reminded of high school. It was a modern government institution, and so everything had been built in the name of efficiency. The lighting, the floors, the chairs all felt like high school. The prisoners weren't wearing stripes or handcuffs, there were no bars on the doors, and the guards didn't walk down concrete halls with their footsteps echoing as they whistled ominously and ran their batons across the cell doors. The prisoners went about doing different tasks like anyone does throughout their day. I could almost see myself forgetting that I was actually in prison. There are lots of places that you can't leave whenever you want: cruise ships, Space Mountain, most jobs. What was most striking for me about visiting prison was that from the inside it felt like just another place to hang out.

The yard itself was an enormous ugly octagon. There was poorly maintained grass in the center and around the edges were concrete walkways covered in bird shit. The whole complex felt like something that cost a lot of money, money that could go towards other, more enjoyable parts of society. At the same time it felt like money was purposely spent there to intimidate and belittle instead of to raise and inspire. Which of course it was.

Jim led us around, more doors locking behind us in a very thorough way. He left us alone to set up our gear in a tiny concrete room while he fetched the inmates. If you were prone to claustrophobia or panic attacks, if you let your mind wander about what a power outage or a riot or a total breakdown of order would be like in there—well, it was best to keep your mind from going there. When the inmates came in they were not shackled or restrained. They had the look about them of people who had been told where to go and what to do for so long that they didn't have any velocity anymore. Kindergarteners who are shuffled along a pathway in a similarly regimented way look like they could randomly run off the path any second and upset all that adult order. Prisoners are always depicted in film and television as being full of rage and danger. In reality all their power has been taken away. There is nothing to be gained from pushing against the system. By this point they are smoothed-down stones.

Our first show together as a quartet took place at nine in the morning. It's hard for most musicians to feel warmed-up and ready to play music early in the day, but especially so when your audience is a mental ward. Though the men were docile, some of them were eggs scrambled in their shells. A man with big bushy eyebrows sat in the audience with his arms folded and made twitchy sexual gestures at my new violinist. "Have you guys read anything good lately?" I asked. "*Playboy*," was the response. Whenever I was stuck for something to say, which was often, I'd turn to Dorota and tell everyone how she was a scientist and was traveling to Antarctica that winter to dive under the ice and study bugs.

The allure of Folsom Prison, of course, is due to Johnny Cash, who wrote a song called "Folsom Prison Blues" about a man who shot another man "just to watch him die." Johnny was never actually locked up in Folsom or any other prison. He first heard about Folsom when he was in the Air Force and watched the film *Inside the Walls of Folsom Prison*. The audience on his live album *At Folsom Prison* sounds a lot rowdier than any I experienced. Of course, by 1968, when he recorded it, Johnny was a world-class star. Imagine spending your life in confinement and getting to see one of the best performers in the world, someone whose songs you knew.

Johnny was in prime form in Folsom. The environment injects a unique energy into every part of his performance. It makes you wonder why more live albums aren't recorded in places where the performer feels a little uncomfortable.

The response to our second gig of the day was much warmer. We played in a library to forty or so men. From the moment we began setting up they were politely curious about us. One of them even asked if we liked the band The Lumineers. From his perspective we were playing the same genre of music, especially compared with everything else on the Grammys. We explained that we actually knew the band personally, but these men didn't seem to believe us. This led to the question of why we weren't performing on the Grammys. A very earnest and well-intentioned man raised his hand. "At what point did you realize that you weren't going to be successful at music?" he wanted to know.

Everyone in the room kind of winced at the question, but I knew what he meant. You can't fake fame. Either someone has heard of you or they haven't. Even these prisoners had heard of The Lumineers. I told him that I've learned to gauge success by my ability to keep doing the projects that I want to do, that all I've ever really wanted to do is play music with people I love. Ideally people will listen and I'll still have enough money to feed myself and travel the world. As long as these are my circumstances, I will consider myself a success. Some of the prisoners started nodding as I was talking, including a thoughtful-looking man in the back with a goatee. He had a knit cap on and I'd like to imagine that his nickname was Ice Man. When I finished my speech about the true meaning of success he chimed in by saying, "And that's *your* Grammy." For a moment, it felt like we were in an inspirational prison movie where we'd thought we were teaching the prisoners something, but really they were teaching *us*. Tears, hugs, freeze-frame.

It turned out to be one of the most civilized, dignified gigs I've ever played. We could tell how much it meant to them that they got to hear live music. Most adventures in playing live music are tests of your willingness to debase yourself. There was none of that in the library in Folsom.

All four shows were much more interactive and conversational than a typical show in a bar full of free adults. For one, nobody had a cellphone to worry over. I finished playing my song "A Narrow Way," and after everyone clapped a man sitting in the front row said, "Say that last line again."

So I recited it to him:

> Ten million kisses on a statue leave a dent
> every pair of lips takes away a piece of sediment
> it is slow
> but it means so much more to me
> than all the words you said when we were in love

"What does that mean?" he asked. I told him that it was about how your devotion to someone can slowly wear that person down, that needing something from someone has a way of diminishing them. I told him it was about following someone down a path that I thought was right, and only after I had gone too far did I realize that it was wrong, but it had looked so right for so much of the time I was on it. I started to hesitate a bit as I said this, knowing that words about regret carried much more weight in a place where everyone had all day every day to think about their mistakes.

It was only inside that I started to notice how many times I mention prison in my songs. There I was, with no real knowledge of prison, using prison metaphors in front of actual prisoners. It made me scrutinize the motives behind my metaphors.

Intellectually I react to prison the same way I react to war, neither of which I've actually experienced. It's incredible to me that the same creatures with the tenderness and nuance to produce Chopin's "Preludes" and Picasso's "Seated Woman" can effectively say, "The best way to solve arguments is to drop big metal objects on towns and the best way to deal with lawbreakers is to put them in stone boxes."

I'm not advocating that we swing the prison doors open wide, but I'm disturbed by how little we think about why we lock people up. As I walked around and met the inmates at Folsom I kept thinking, *This doesn't seem right.* Prison in its modern incarnation still feels more like a temporary solution, one that has been around for hundreds of years.

Adam Gopnik wrote in *The New Yorker*, "Mass incarceration on a scale almost unexampled in human history is a fundamental fact of our country today—perhaps the fundamental fact, as slavery was the fundamental fact of 1850. In truth, there are more black men in the grip of the criminal-justice system—in prison, on probation, or on parole—than were in slavery then. Overall, there are now more people under 'correctional supervision' in America—more than six million—than were in the Gulag Archipelago under Stalin at its height."

When you're interacting with them, you don't know what the inmates have done to wind up in prison. You probably don't want to know. You could never know all the circumstances of how they arrived at their own particular horrifying moment anyway. It's not like they have nametags telling their story, and it's not like they're just going to bring it up. I sure didn't feel like I was in a position to ask. Only later did our guide let us in on some of the prisoners' stories. One of the men who had said our music was really pretty (and who suggested that we should call our band "Jes-us" with a hyphen) had killed his parents because he was tormented by demons and was trying to free their souls.

A few of the prisoners were songwriters and wanted to play their songs for us. After we finished our set in the library, we went to a little room where they kept the musical instruments. A prisoner named Marty played us a song called "Chains," a very literal song about the regret he felt about being locked up, every bit as heartbreaking as you could imagine such a song to be. I found out later that Marty was having trouble because he wasn't affiliated with any gang. Transferring to another prison wasn't much of an option. Prisoners would sometimes kill a new transfer if they thought he was too soft.

An older man named Ken picked up an electric guitar that wasn't plugged into anything and played a jazz tune he wrote called "C'est La Vie," about a woman who repeatedly spurns a man's advances in every verse until the end of the song when she finally decides that she wants him. "You're too late, baby," he says. "C'est la vie." I found out later that Ken had been in Folsom for thirty years. One terrible night in the early eighties he came home and found his wife having sex with another man. He killed both of them in a fury and had been sitting in prison ever since. Marty played another song while Ken sat there with the electric guitar in his lap. In between verses he played an unamplified blues solo that was everything blues is supposed to be and never is, full of frustrated wrong notes. Marty's voice cut through the sunniness of the day. "I don't want to die with no one knowing I was here."

It shouldn't be more important to play to fashionable young people in hip cities than it is to play for men who have heard very little live music in decades. I mean, I understand why playing for fashionable people is more important for my career and my possible dating life, but the experience means so much less to them than it means to the men who never get to hear music. It could be argued that since prisoners rarely get to hear live music, it's not much of a compliment if they like mine. Any band could come into that prison and play any old music and probably change some lives, but that doesn't make it any less valuable.

The next day we played two more shows. The first one was again in a small room in the mental ward. As we stood there and watched the prisoners file in, one of them got really riled up and tried to talk to the recreational therapist who was holding open the door. The prisoner was upset about something that had happened in the yard.

"Man, I'm so mad about what he did—"

"We'll talk about it later."

"But I'm really pissed."

"Sit down and watch the show. We'll talk about it after."

After we played music for an hour and the prisoners were filing out, the therapist asked the man what he wanted to talk about. The prisoner looked surprised for a second.

"Man, after listening to that music, I forget what I was mad about."

At our last show a band of prisoners opened for us. A man named Adam played electric guitar while his friend played an electronic drum set with the volume turned down so as not to be disruptive. In the middle of the set Adam said that his friends had made him a T-shirt for his birthday and had dared him to wear it. He tore open his prison-issued jacket. The shirt had been cut into ribbons at the waist. "ROCK STAR," it said, with pink stars around the letters. They had made it to embarrass him, but he'd decided to embrace it.

After the set, a man named Drifter asked how he could get ahold of my music. He gave me a pen and paper and I started writing down my website. "We don't have the Internet here," he said.

On our way out of the prison, we had to wait in a small vestibule for a few minutes with a group of medical personnel and an empty stretcher. They were joking around and seemed really light-hearted. I turned to John to make a joke. John was staring at the stretcher. I looked back at it and noticed a bulge that looked like it could have been a pair of feet. Then I saw what could have been a head, and then I realized that it wasn't an empty stretcher, but the dead body of a prisoner. They made sure to check his ID on the way out, but his body was finally allowed to leave the prison.

I wondered about his final days. Maybe while watching the Grammys he had imagined that he was in that fancy audience or up on the stage. Maybe he dreamt that he was a sailor circling the globe. You can't lock up the human mind so you have to lock up the body, but as soon as the mind and spirit are gone the body can leave. It makes all the sense in the world and yet when we got out of the prison and drove home in silence, really thinking about it, it didn't make sense at all. None of it did.

# *Ten*

It is 9:45 p.m. at the meditation retreat, a criminal time to have to go to sleep for people who get excited by darkness. I comfort myself by thinking of a video I have watched so many times on YouTube I can picture it with my eyes closed. It is from *The Johnny Cash Show,* a variety show that ran from 1969 to 1971. It was recorded at the Ryman Theater in Nashville and gave Johnny the chance to be country music's ambassador to the rest of America. Country music today is so wrapped up in the politics of laying claim to a particular set of American values that it's hard to believe there was a time when it was seen as a way of uniting the country.

On September 23rd, 1970, Johnny and his wife June are onstage talking. She says that she regrets having missed time from the show because of giving birth to their son, as though he were a cold she foolishly caught from running around in the rain. She then recites a really strange and corny poem about milking a cow. After some uncomfortable moments, this earns a laugh from the audience. Upon finishing she looks deep into Johnny's eyes while he praises her. "Was that okay?" she keeps asking. Johnny keeps saying, "You did good." "Was it?" she asks again. "You did good."

Johnny announces that the next guest will be Ray Charles. Johnny sits on the piano bench next to Ray. He reveals that it's Ray's fortieth birthday. "On behalf of the Country Music Association," he continues, "I want to say thanks to you for taking country music around the world and introducing it to a lot of people. Nashville welcomes you with open arms." Coming from a man who was at the time the king of country music, it must have felt like being knighted.

Ray looks very touched and says he has something to play for Johnny. He begins an impromptu solo version of "Walk The Line." After a verse and a chorus he stops and says, "Did you hear that?"

"Yes, that's something else," Johnny says.

Then Johnny mentions that Ray has a new album of country songs called *Love Country Style.* Ray Charles laughs and says, "You know that city love ain't quite like country style."

"No, it's a little bit different," Johnny says, and everyone laughs knowingly.

For a place that once endured an actual, bloody Civil War, it's strange to think of how the real divisions in the United States have always been more about country versus city. It's even stranger to think that something so fluid and ambiguous as music could be caught up in those dividing lines, but as Ray Charles is about to demonstrate, those divisions have nothing to do with words, chords, and melodies.

Ray says, "Well, here's a little song called 'Ring of Fire.'"

He says the title of the song like it burns his mouth. He supposedly kicked heroin in 1966. The way his body is pulsing, it looks more like he's on cocaine. I can almost see the electricity coursing through his body, and every word he says is delivered with a delicious joy. If he is on drugs, it is quite an argument for doing drugs.

The song begins with a large unseen band backing Ray. They have a very groovy seventies feel, light years away from the Mariachi-influenced country folk of the original. When Ray sings one line and leaves a space that was normally occupied by a horn line in Cash's version, there's just this big deep groove into which we can push all of our secret physical urges.

The most compelling moment comes at the breakdown after the first chorus. Ray stops playing piano and looks up with joy and just spasms for a few seconds as the bass line keeps going. He lets out an "Aghh," and then comes in right with the band. If you notated this moment musically on a score, there would be nothing in Ray's part except for several rests, and yet it is one of the most fascinating things I've ever seen a musician do. He is just silently convulsing with the rhythm as though doing so were more important than any notes he could play. Wherever he is, the invisible bass player seems taken aback, and even begins to lose the tempo, but then Ray comes back in and syncs up with the big brass hits.

He delights in every word of the lyrics, reveling in the sensuality of them. It's odd to think that the song was written by June Carter after seeing a page in her uncle's book of Elizabethan poetry. The burning referenced the fires of hell that you fall into when you succumb to desire, the kind of desire she felt for Johnny, who was married at the time.

Or did Johnny actually write the song? Johnny's first wife Vivian Liberto claims as much in her book *I Walked The Line*: "To this day, it confounds me to hear the elaborate details June told of writing that song for Johnny. She didn't write that song any more than I did. The truth is, Johnny wrote that song, while piled up and drunk, about a certain female body part. All those years of her claiming she wrote it herself, and she probably never knew what the song was really about."

It's pretty unusual when there's a question of song ownership between two lovers. It's not like you ever have to wonder if Eric Clapton or Pattie Boyd wrote "Layla."

If the subtext of the song really was about a certain female body part, Ray takes that subtext and explodes it all over the Ryman.

On the last chorus he gets really quiet and starts to sound a little unearthly. "That ring of fire, that ring of fire," he chants. Then his voice falls to just an ominous whisper: "It burns, burns, burns, that ring of fire."

As the band behind him dies out, Ray is still going, like he doesn't want the song to end, and he lets out one last shudder and cackle like he just invented the orgasm, "Burns. Ah- ha- ha- ha."

The crowd gives a standing ovation and Johnny returns to the stage, looking like a man who just watched someone have sex with his wife, but was so in awe of how good he was at it that he could only thank him.

# *Eleven*

I'm in awe of that moment because I know how hard it can be to locate that sexuality, not to mention be *confident* about it. Sometimes you meet a new person and are just totally turned off, and it's not because of their smell and it's not because of their personality and it's not even because of their objective "hotness" but rather, you suspect, it's embedded deep in their DNA, like there was a time thousands of years ago when glaciers were receding and your ancestors' tribe passed a very similar but still different tribe on a European steppe and an elder from your tribe made it clear with his body language that it was not okay to mate with someone from that tribe, like not just not okay in a romantic Romeo and Juliet way, but not okay in a *we'll gore you with our primitive spears and throw you in a crevasse* kind of way, and that fear of goring was stored in your ancestor's DNA and carried down to you, so that all it takes now is approximately one-eighth of a second on an OkCupid date for you to recognize that it's just not going to go anywhere, but maybe it's rude to walk out on a date after only one-eighth of a second.

There was no overt talk of sex in my house when I was young. When I was nine I watched *Purple Rain* with my parents. I'll never forget that uncomfortable moment when Apollonia takes her clothes off and jumps in Lake Minnetonka. It was the first time I had seen a naked woman, the first time I'd seen those *things* she had. That night the image of her kept me awake, even though I didn't know what the other parts really looked like.

A few years later when my voice was changing, my mom left a copy of *What's Happening to Me?* at my door without comment. The book consisted of cartoon drawings of people going through changes and trying to understand sex. This approach was probably a little too cute; some aspects could have been explained more explicitly. Sexual intercourse, I learned from the book, was a moment when two people were naked in the dark and rubbed up against each other until there was a big "POP." What was the pop? How did it happen simultaneously between two people? I wondered about that for a long time.

And I still wonder if you can identify the exact moment you fall in love with someone. If you plotted your affections for someone on a timeline, a colorful poster board presentation with a big gray area labeled "not in love" and a big yellow area labeled "in love," it seems to me that there must be some moment when you cross over from one area to the next. For me, with Melanie, it was when she asked me to help her take off her Chinese gown.

This was after I had married and divorced Amanda, but was still living in the house on Emerson Street in which the two of us had lived. I had moved down to the basement and Melanie lived on the second floor, next to Amanda. The divorce was necessary and amicable, but it still felt a little odd to be hanging out with Melanie in that house. One night Melanie and I met up at a party that we had both agreed to dress up for—me the best I could with a shirt and tie, she in a beautiful shiny silk gown she bought when she was in China. We came back to the house after the party and talked in the kitchen for a long time, still in our nice clothes. I wanted the conversation to keep going, even though it was late. It reached its end and she said goodnight and went up to her bedroom. I felt the emptiness of that moment, the night suddenly over. I was about to walk down to my basement room with my chin on my chest when she came back down the stairs and said, "Can you help me take this gown off? It's too tight."

We didn't kiss at all that night, but we continued to hang out for weeks. One night, while Amanda was out of town visiting her new boyfriend, I slept in our old bedroom. I had a fitful night of sleep knowing Melanie was just a few feet away. I got up to go to the bathroom in the middle of the night, and as I walked back to the room, I saw Melanie standing outside her bedroom in a white muu-muu, floating there, as if she were created to stand right there at that quiet moment in human history. It was just a coincidence that she'd gotten up to use the bathroom at the same time. She looked like a benevolent ghost who could see into the future and tell me how to avoid danger. She looked like every idea of sex I ever had, Apollonia diving into the lake and the pop in the dark. I wasn't even really sure if she was actually standing there.

That moment stretched out forever, me stunned by her sudden presence, us finding each other at 3:47 a.m. or whenever. In reality it was probably only a few seconds. It would have been all right, I suppose, if I had walked right up and kissed her that night, both of us drunk on the surreal possibilities. Instead I went back to my empty bed and buried myself in months of regret.

Melanie later told me about the moment that she fell for me. I was in the kitchen talking with her and Lori one afternoon and we noticed how the clock on the wall hadn't been set forward since Daylight Savings Time. Melanie took the clock off the wall and it slipped out of her hands. It fell on the floor, and in a burst of whimsy I jumped on it as soon as it hit the floor, assuming that it was already going to be broken. I kicked it with my foot and yelled out, "Stupid clock! Die!" Melanie laughed as though I were a catatonic madman who suddenly sprang into action for no reason. Plot that moment on the timeline in bright yellow paper.

Shortly after that, Melanie took a job in Los Angeles and moved out of the house. Nothing overtly romantic had happened between us. I'd have to wait.

Dear __________,

"Don't be afraid of change," you once told me. "The things you love had to change to get to the point where they were lovable to you."

We were in the produce aisle. You waved at the display of Cameo apples and said, "These all used to be flowers."

I went swimming in the Gulf of Mexico the other day. You can wade out for about three quarters of a mile and the water is still just waist deep. Looking back at the shore, you can't distinguish your friends from the trashcans. There is a long line of wooden poles spaced a hundred feet apart out there marking the point where the water finally gets deep. It's kind of scary to walk up to them, these tall poles with pelicans resting on top, stretching their long necks. As you approach them, you begin to worry that there is too much ocean behind you. What would happen if you took a step, only to find nothing there? You would be swept away while the pelicans go on stretching their long necks.

I suppose that's what falling in love feels like.

Trying not to slip,
Nick

# *Twelve*

I'VE ALWAYS BEEN DRAWN to the places that scare me the most, the parts of the map where the lines trail off and serpents fill the rest of the page. I like to imagine the mapmakers shrugging and saying, "Well, we're not sure what's over this hill. Probably serpents."

I'm interested in the kind of city that is not on a map. Maps can only document what has already been seen, and I've always wanted to go somewhere that has never been seen. I created an entire New Orleans in my mind before I ever went there. In some ways it was a naïve construction, but I miss that imaginary city. I first went to New Orleans because of a dream. But it was someone else's dream.

It was 1997 and I was biking around Ireland listening to a cassette of Paul Simon's musical *The Capeman.* I decided I wanted to write my own musical when I got back to California. I knew how to write songs, but I had never written a story before. One evening I sat with my guitar in my parents' living room and started strumming chords and singing nonsense words. The first line that came out was, "Oh, when I die they won't even bury me." *What the hell does that mean?* I thought. *What person would be so pathetic that he wouldn't even be buried?*

I was about to move on to something else when my friend David called. He's a screenwriter who looks kind of like Ethan Hawke in *Before Sunrise*. He is intense and steeped in story. "What are you doing?" he asked. "Oh, just trying to start this musical," I said. If I were talking to anyone else, I probably wouldn't have said more. "I'm trying to think of a story. All I have so far is this one line, but it's nothing." "What is it?" he asked. "I don't even know what it means," I told him. "'Oh when I die, they won't even bury me.'"

There was a pause. "That's funny," David said. Then another pause. "I just read something about how in New Orleans they don't bury bodies in the ground because the water table is so high that they'll just seep back up to the surface. And it's weird, because even though I've never been there, I had a dream about New Orleans last night. I was watching a funeral parade through the streets with a big crowd, and when it got dark, the coffin lid popped open and the body inside jumped out and ran away, and everyone chased after it." He paused again. "I didn't even realize it until just now, but the person that jumped out of the coffin was you."

So there I had in one dream my directive for the next year: write and record a musical that led up to that climactic image, and then find a way to New Orleans. I stayed up every night working on it and slept during the day. I would head to the university library in the hours before closing to look at travel books about the city. I put into New Orleans all my hopes for what I was missing from my own life. New loves are always the receptacles for all those impossible wishes.

Maybe you're tracking the scent of sweet jasmine or you only feel alive in places with heat lightning and Spanish moss; all of us are following some trail. I made a song out of Jacques Prévert's "Chanson des Escargots Qui Vont a L'Enterrement," a poem in which two snails go to a dead leaf's funeral. They start out in the autumn, and because they are so slow they don't get there until the spring. By that time everything is alive again, so they drink beer and sing songs and stumble home happy. How French, to think that if you take it slow enough everything will get better.

Eventually, I met a girl heading to New Orleans who let me ride along in her van. I had studied French poetry because I knew there was a profound French influence in the city, but upon arrival I realized that in New Orleans they pronounce beautiful French words like they're slamming the door on a soufflé. Actual French people must be garroted to see their delicate language so mispronounced.

Every time I'm away for a while the dream New Orleans swirls back into my memory, and when I go to the real New Orleans there is a swift end to that dream when I am faced with the savage truth of the city. What I always forget is that the reason New Orleans is so committed to letting the good times roll is because it lives so closely with death. One time I came back to town to see photocopied "MISSING" signs posted on telephone poles, on them the face of a young father who was last seen wading in the Mississippi. After a couple weeks the signs were bleached from the sun and peeling off. His body never surfaced. Another time, just a few months after Katrina, my friend Gill told me how several days earlier he'd ordered a pizza and chatted with the delivery guy for a few minutes. The next day the delivery guy jumped off the top floor of the Omni Royal Orleans Hotel. When the police entered his home they found that he'd chopped his girlfriend up and put her in pots on the stove.

I try to turn away from such stories, but they are there in New Orleans more than they are in most places.

But that is what gives New Orleans such life. Sit in just about any bar and write on a napkin things you overhear and you'll already have the beginnings of a song.

"If that doesn't work, I'll just go back to L.A. and make the same damn film everyone else makes." "We used to flirt with each other backstage at Camelot, and when we'd leg wrestle I'd notice the weird homemade patches on her jeans."

Ride your bicycle through Marigny and the French Quarter, weaving your way through delivery trucks and tourists. You will see at least one person dressed like he or she is crazy who will be making a lot of money, and many people dressed like they make a lot of money who will be acting crazy. It is a place where you can pretend that consequences don't exist, like that magical time when you were young and you got on the carousel with your brother while your mom waited on the side. You spun around knowing that someone was holding your bag for you, holding your place in the real world. As Charles Broome said to me once during a funeral parade on Frenchmen Street, "Time in New Orleans is more crooked than Einstein could have ever dreamed."

Find the coffee shop near the Central Business District where the concrete floor slopes subtly upward making it so—this is such a New Orleans thing—the door doesn't open easily because it scrapes against the ground. Don't fuss with it, because there's nothing that can be done; it's just an inherently difficult door to open. Sit there for an hour watching different people approach the door and push on it, then do that thing where they think something is wrong or they're being tricked, until they remember that it's New Orleans and they just resume pushing it while looking slightly embarrassed. Sit there until a woman walks in inexplicably holding a couch pillow. She will have trouble opening the door and look over at you bemusedly until she finally succeeds. She'll spend only about thirty seconds looking around the coffee shop before wrestling with the door on her way out. She'll manage it with Buster Keaton-like humor, and look at you through the window with a knowing smile as she starts to walk away. If you're lucky, she'll stop walking and come back and push the door open again just so she can remind you, "Nothing's easy, is it?"

Dear ________,

The entirety of humankind's quest towards more efficient technology has been about reassembling the world from the outside in. We saw a hummingbird and dreamed of a helicopter. We saw the motion of matter in magical states and we charted it on the Periodic Table. Now we see a tiger and divide it into smaller and smaller grids in which colored pixels can represent the pieces of a tiger and those pieces can be transmitted onto a screen and look almost exactly like a tiger.

When we were in that strip club a couple months ago, your sister told me that every man she had ever dated had been afraid of her. Including the nice guy who had treated her right and who she perhaps uncourteously dumped in favor of a guy who seems to me and to you and to everyone else like a total asshole, but this asshole is, at last, a guy who isn't afraid of her, she said. And that was worth more to her than the kindness and reciprocity of a nice man's love. I understand that. I've been on that side of it too. Being with someone who is afraid of you is like being followed by your own shadow, knowing that it can never surprise you or challenge you. It's cruel, but when you have the upper hand in a relationship you can get complacent. So some of us end up looking for someone who is complacent with us, who treats us like we're his or her shadow. Why do we chase the creatures that are indifferent to us? Why do we adore the face that doesn't break? Why do we wrap ourselves up in masking tape on that living room stage, like your sister did in that seaside lodge, in a state of complete what-the-fuckness over someone who finally isn't afraid of us?

I was afraid of you. Afraid that when you got up to go to the restroom you'd never come back. Afraid that you'd never return my call. I told myself I deserved to feel this way, because I've been on the other side of that. I've punished people who cared too much about me. I've laughed at their dramatic gestures. I've had nothing on the line.

With you, I was the shadow. There was nowhere else I could have moved, nothing I could have done that would have changed the outcome. Shadows have no power.

Regretting the actions that led to where we are now is like trying to reassemble a tiger from the outside in, hoping that it will still be a tiger. There is a breath and a spirit to real life that can never be captured in all the smaller and smaller divisions. That spirit is what we should be trying to capture. The particulars of the tiger are irrelevant. If you were to actually encounter a tiger out in the wild, really face a tiger, you would soon forget the exact placement of the stripes, the shape of its nose, the alignment of its whiskers, but you'd never forget the tiger. You'd remember all the unquantifiable bits. Your hair would stand on end and you'd know that what was happening was real. Maybe that's why we're looking for someone we're afraid of, because our fear tells us that we are real, whereas complacency makes us feel like we are disappearing. Of course there's always the possibility that the tiger might devour us and then we'll become just another piece of the tiger.

Yours in reality,
Nick

# *Thirteen*

I AM SITTING in a white plastic chair warming my hands on a cup of Inka and my face in the last rays of the setting sun. With some time to myself before the group reassembles in the hall, I am once again listening to *Graceland.*

The first dozen times I heard the title song I didn't know what Paul Simon meant when he referred to the Mississippi Delta shining like a National guitar. It just seemed like a bland lyric about some metaphorical guitar that represented the whole nation. I realized later that a National brand guitar is a guitar made out of metal that has big resonators on it so that it projects sound. A metal guitar shines in the spotlights the way a river does in the sunset.

Paul Simon remythologized a place that had already been thoroughly mythologized. The song and the album are not really about Elvis, and yet they are about the world that Elvis helped bring about. Graceland, the actual place, cannot possibly stand up to the mythology. The idea that you're going to commune with Elvis in his own home is a very odd concept. Perhaps someday we'll see the same thing with Neverland Ranch. I've never understood the fetishizing of the particulars of a person who happened to create great music. Does it help your understanding of the song "Suspicious Minds" to see all the mirrors on the stairway to the basement?

When I went to Graceland, the most disingenuous part of the experience was that they kept the upstairs off limits under the illusion that some things needed to remain private. It seemed a little late for this man to retain his privacy, and for the thirty-six dollars it took to get in you'd think they would turn out every cupboard and give you a flashlight to inspect the foundation if you wanted to. At the same time it did leave the contents of his bedroom to the imagination, which is probably the best place for it. Nothing that was actually up there would surpass our expectations. I enjoyed picturing Elvis himself upstairs, feeling under the weather, holding a towel over his head while steaming water leached the toxins from his pores. The message was that Elvis would be back. Or he never left.

# Fourteen

NINA SIMONE WALKS ONSTAGE at the Montreux Jazz Festival and sits at a Bösendorfer grand piano.

"This song is popular all over France and with Chanel No. 5 perfume," she says. "Unfortunately, of which, I have none, and not the money either."

This evening in Switzerland she doesn't look particularly happy. She mostly looks tired. Nina is, like many musicians, never happy with her level of success. She feels like she should have had a hit song, sold more records, played to bigger crowds. That burning resentment is always present in her, making every song choice she makes tonight seem monumental.

"It's from our first album, the very first album we made in this world, which is at least twenty-five years old."

Her voice gives a gasp of wonder as she says the number of years, as though she can't believe a quarter century has passed since she recorded this song. It's 1987.

"I only wish I was as wise—could have been as wise then—as I have become now. I have suffered."

These are harrowing words to say, and she bows her head under their weight. How often does a performer on stage burst out with such a frank admission of her place in life? To admit to suffering like this is no different than wearing a sign listing all her failures as a human being.

Among these failures, in her mind at least, is the inability to have a stable relationship. She has been abused, both physically and financially. Despite her ferocity as a performer, she has never been strong enough to be her own source of stability, and so she has constantly suffered the consequences, whether they come in the form of fists or financial ruin. At this particular moment in 1987 she looks like she is surveying all of her personal history, which makes what should be a simple introduction to a crowd-pleasing song at a world-renowned jazz festival in Switzerland much more complicated. She gathers herself after that last confession to finish her setup to the song.

"But there is a Bösendorfer here, so we'll see what happens."

Almost as though, if there weren't a Bösendorfer there, things would be different. Like if she had walked out to find that it was just a Yamaha, would she go, "You know what? Forget it."

This is the chance we take when we witness seminal performers: the possibility of an incendiary testimonial of truth is equal to the possibility that they might just not be in the mood and bail on the moment. Tonight, Nina is in *some* mood. Anything could happen.

She launches into the familiar riff to "My Baby Just Cares for Me." It's in a higher register than the popular recording, at a much faster tempo. It is only recognizable for the first fifteen seconds or so, and then she starts to play variations on top of the chord progression. She plays the keys very quietly, as though she were entertaining nobility in a fancy parlor and trying not to startle anyone.

When she starts singing the words, it sounds like she's singing them just to herself, the way you would when you're rehearsing a song and trying to remember the lines. It's as though she has forgotten that there is an audience.

When she gets to the line, "Liz Taylor is not his style, and even Sally Burton's smile is something he can't see," she stifles a smile. She's spontaneously inserted the name of Richard Burton's widow in the same line with the woman he married and divorced twice. The relief from the sadness—the creative joy—is visible. She nods her head playfully when she gets to the words "high-toned places," and we can tell she is now fully inhabiting the song.

After the second chorus she launches into an extended musical interlude that lasts about three minutes. The thrilling piano solo of the original is completely abandoned for a jagged contrapuntal journey. Again, we are at a much faster tempo than the original. Where that old version had a sultry jazz swing to it, this one has a complicated classical feel. Her playing exhibits breathtaking dynamics, fully exploring everything that the Bösendorfer can do.

At one point in the middle of the solo she starts to sing the next verse, then shakes her head as if she's a pitcher waving off a bad sign from the catcher. The solo has taken over.

It's hard to encapsulate exactly how incredible what she's doing here is. She is playing very fast and precise Bach-style contrapuntal inventions. Whether these are improvised or planned out is not clear. It certainly feels like the horizontal structure of the song is elastic, since she can make the solo as long as she feels like making it. She is doing all of this world-class classical piano playing while also singing the song in her distinct bluesy voice. The styles are so different that if you only heard the audio you would have to imagine that it was two different people performing it, probably in different eras entirely.

I can imagine a lot of people in the audience are disappointed to hear such a different rendition. However, this is a jazz festival, and this is what jazz musicians are supposed to do: create music that is alive.

After all, this is a fifty-four-year-old black American living in France playing a song that is older than her and imbuing it with the hallmarks of a German composer born three centuries ago. This is not just another run-through of a hit song from a perfume commercial.

Consider the original version, written by Walter Donaldson and Gus Kahn for the 1930 film *Whoopee!* It is fairly horrifying to watch Eddie Cantor prance around in blackface doing the whitest dance moves possible as a group of bemused white women in enormous cowboy hats look on. You feel ashamed for being within a hundred years of it. In the original version of the song the lyrics go, "But Rodgers is not her style, and even Chevalier's smile," which referred to Richard Rodgers, from the songwriting team of Rodgers and Hart and later Rodgers and Hammerstein, and the French actor Maurice Chevalier.

Nina Simone recorded the song in 1958, updating the names in the process. Liz Taylor had just starred in *Giant* with James Dean, and Lana Turner had starred in *Peyton Place* with Lee Philips. So it goes "Liz Taylor is not his style, and even Lana Turner's smile," until the last verse, when she substitutes "Liberace" for "Lana Turner," an interesting gender twist. It's funny to think of the kind of man she would be singing about who might consider both herself and Liberace as romantic possibilities.

The song wasn't a hit initially. In fact it wasn't very popular until 1987 when it was used in a Chanel No. 5 perfume commercial in the U.K. As Nina mentions, she didn't benefit financially from this arrangement.

I first heard the song at *Spike & Mike's Twisted Animation Festival* at the Crest Theater in Sacramento. I was maybe ten years old, and I thought it was so cool and subversive to be watching cartoons that weren't Bugs Bunny. I remember in particular a claymation short of this song depicting Nina Simone as a female cat. It was created by Aardman Studios (which went on to make *Wallace and Gromit*) and the animation looks clumsy by their standards. I remember the piano solo being so exciting because the audience seemed to fall into the instrument and rattle around with the keys. What it unfortunately led me to believe was that the singer and the piano player were two different creatures.

Chanel No. 5 turned the song into a standard, the kind of song that singers mindlessly put into their sets to please audiences.

Here is Natalie Cole performing it at a televised concert in London in 2002. We're worlds away from Montreux. Everyone in the band is dressed in tuxedos and the audience is sitting at cocktail tables with little lamps at each. "This next song is really, really old," Natalie Cole says, as though the other songs she sings are not. She gives the history of its evolution from *Whoopee!* to her father Nat King Cole singing it, coyly trying to conceal its identity for a minute.

Then she mentions that the most popular version was "probably" by Nina Simone. And then, knowing that the audience can guess what the song is by now, she cornily says, "The song goes something like this. A very cool song."

As the enormous soft jazz orchestra starts the song behind her she cajoles them to "Come on," as though that would get them to play with any more spirit. The band is full of polish and absolutely no personality. All the life is gone from the song by the time the verse kicks in. It's just something you listen to while you shop for Christmas presents. Natalie Cole makes silly jazzy gestures as she sings, undermining the torment of real performers like Nina. It's music for people that don't like to feel things.

At Montreux in 1987, there is a moment in Nina's piano interlude when the song almost comes to a halt. She has established the main chord structure and all the variations so solidly that now she can abandon rhythm and harmony for a few measures to just punctuate a few notes.

When she finally comes in with the last verse it looks like she's crying. The piano is rolling, having built up so much energy from all the crests and valleys she has dragged it through. She again sounds like she's singing just for herself. The piano comes to an incredible roar, and her voice finally bursts out to acceptable stage volume with, "High-toned places," and the song climaxes with her hands far apart on the Bösendorfer, extracting a symphony's worth of sound from one instrument.

The whole piece lasts seven minutes and every second is baffling. At the end of the performance she has the exhausted look of a grandmother whose grandchildren were able to convince her to tell a story for the hundredth time. She gazes at the audience with a look of, "There. Are you happy now?"

# *Fifteen*

ONLY AFTER SEVERAL DAYS of meditation am I certain that I have the track listing to The Beatles' *White Album* right. If I were in the normal world I would've looked it up on the Internet in a matter of seconds, but there is some hard-earned satisfaction in spending three days of my life trying to remember if "Glass Onion" is really the third song. I kept thinking it sounded right coming out of "Dear Prudence," but then I would wonder, *They wouldn't put such a weird song like that so early on, would they?*

I remember years ago listening to the song "Everybody's Got Something to Hide Except Me and My Monkey" on headphones and hearing a flubbed guitar note. I had to rewind the song and listen again to make sure. It was so exciting to hear a mistake in something so canonical. I heard another flub in the song "Maxwell's Silver Hammer" when Paul laughed while singing the line about Maxwell staying behind after class. I made a list of all the mistakes in Beatles' songs, and they became my favorite parts, the moments where you could tell that real people were in a room making this music.

You're probably not supposed to do this in meditation, think about the track listing of *The White Album*.

Dear __________,

When you drove me home that one night from swing dancing I asked you how it felt to dance with such ease and grace. You told me that it depended on the partner. You said, "Sometimes a man puts his hand on me and I can just feel his neediness, and it's harder to enjoy myself."

You told me once about how hard it is to move on from a broken heart because of all the unavoidable reminders of that person you loved. Certain holidays, or that Walkmen song, or the Monopolowa and soda they always ordered. You said that with your ex-fiancé, what came back were the jasmine flowers that were blooming on the trip the two of you made to India. To avoid thinking about what you lost isn't as simple as just not going back to India. It's harder than that, because jasmine grows everywhere. So either you'll continue walking around with a constantly broken heart, or maybe you'll just slowly get used to the smell of jasmine in the air, the way a dog from the pound slowly accepts his new home.

Let's not take it so personally that jasmine grows everywhere. Jasmine moves towards sunlight and stretches its roots to grab the moisture in the soil. It's not there to mock you. It's just trying to survive, like everything else.

Yours in full bloom,
Nick

# *Sixteen*

In 2011, when Elizabeth Taylor died at the age of seventy-nine, *The New York Times* published an obituary for her written by a man named Mel Gussow. At the bottom of the article was the surprising footnote that Mr. Gussow himself had died in 2005. Of course it makes sense for a major newspaper to prepare an obituary for a famous person who is nearing the end of her life, but it makes you wonder how much of your own obituary could be written right now, while you're still alive. Have you already done everything you'll be known for? My friend Nathan has always wanted to die by being shot out of a cannon, naked, holding fireworks, so that at least there would be some event that would necessitate a new paragraph in his obituary.

There's a comfort in thinking about all the people anticipating the period at the end of the sentence, and how often they've reached their own ends first. All the people throughout history who have predicted the end of the world have died long before such an event ever happened. Just because something looks like the end of the world doesn't mean that it is. In 1350 about half the population of Europe was killed off by the Black Plague, a disease that manifested itself as boils on the groin and the armpits. Victims would go on to vomit blood in a horrible fever and die within a few days. If half your friends were dying this way, you'd be excused for thinking that this was the end of the world, but it wasn't. Not even remotely. Think of all the great stuff that has happened since 1350. Pretty much everything good: cars, ice cubes, Disneyland, typewriters, flip-flops, Kurt Vonnegut. It's been a nonstop orgy of innovation and fun since that dark time where it seemed like the world might end. Not to rub it in the face of 1350s Europe, but that was so not the end of the world. This probably won't be either.

I saw a billboard on I-10 East in Louisiana that announced in big letters, "MAY 21ST IS JUDGMENT DAY!" and it was referring to The Judgment Day, the judging-of-all-nations-before-God Judgment Day, not some movie or something. It's kind of a funny event to advertise that way, because Judgment Day comes after the Second Coming of Jesus Christ, which is probably a more important date to mention on a big highway billboard. Would that mean He'd be coming on May 20th? Or just earlier on the day of the 21st? The billboard was no different than a high school kid telling all his friends, "My parents come back into town on May 21st!" without telling anyone when the big kegger would be.

The closest I've felt to being at the end of the world was at South by Southwest, the annual music festival in Austin, Texas. I'm aware, of course, that something that happens every year, by definition, can't actually be the end of the world. SXSW does look like a post-apocalyptic hellscape, though, a sort of *Escape from New York*-type world where all the bands on Earth gather in one metropolis and construct a rudimentary society whose hierarchy is determined by the tonnage of one's bass amp, and everyone passes around plastic discs that nobody will ever listen to. From what I've seen there, I suspect that the end of the world is actually going to be pretty tame. Epic parties never end in explosions. They end around dawn, with a couple making out on the couch, their tired feet tracing the stains in the carpet, whatever music that brought them together long since forgotten.

It's weird to be part of something that is ultimately not about spreading art in a meaningful way, but about "making it" or seeing a band before they "made it." If you were a dentist and went to a dental convention, you wouldn't be threatened by how many other people were engaged in the same discipline as you. Everybody needs a dentist. Not everybody needs an indie rock band, and it could be argued that the more indie rock bands you hear, the less special each one becomes.

The thing I have the hardest time with is the sense of entitlement you encounter at SXSW, as if it is written somewhere that by assembling four of your friends and buying guitars and playing power chords while looking at the floor you are owed adulation and wealth. So many crummy bands have been given ridiculous amounts of money to revive the tired corpse of rebellion that used to signify rock music, so I can understand where this idea comes from, but it is still a bummer to witness anyone who believes that the superficial aspects of rock music are the point of the music itself. At one time, turning your amp up and playing simple chords and screaming about something really did threaten the power structure. Unfortunately, that was back in the sixties. Just because loud guitars once signified rebellion doesn't mean that they always will. You have to find ways to subvert people's expectations and do something dangerous that puts them on edge. It's not always going to come from loudness or guitars or distortion or black jeans or skinny dishevelment.

If SXSW is the apocalypse, then *American Idol* is Judgment Day. The idea that there is such a need for "idols" that we must regularly comb every inch of the country for them is really quite fascinating. As a singer, I worry about standing in front of Randy Jackson at the End of Days and having him assess my entire career in terms of marketability and pitch. "Yo dawg, you started out shaky at sixteen, then you kinda got into it in the middle of your career. I didn't really know the songs you were singing, but that's cool, it's kind of a Paul Simon thing you got going on. But you just didn't show us something that we could connect to and the whole thing was kind of pitchy." And that would be it. More humiliating than whatever God could possibly throw at me.

Towards the end of the weekend, I sat on a hill looking down on an indie folk band playing to a small audience. It's rare at SXSW to have a moment when you're not rushing from one of your own gigs to another, to actually have time to take in a show. The singer was nimble and playful and the guitarist was inventive, but their sound was no match for the wind whipping through the stage or the drums and guitars echoing from nearby venues. After they finished, the soundman blasted Michael Jackson's "Rock With You" and everyone got up and danced. All around me was this joyous look of wonder and amazement that I imagine would be recognizable to the liberating Allied forces who rolled into the concentration camps and saw people who had previously lost all hope in humanity. Even though I admired the indie folk band, there's a difference between working to like something and having the music just overtake you. All we wanted was to dance to the greatest dance music ever, something with soul, something that we knew we already liked. All we wanted was a little Michael. Maybe we'd just been waiting for him to die so we could enjoy it again. Maybe when we're all gone, and the ego and creepiness of ambition is removed from the music we're making now, tomorrow's audience won't have so much trouble deciding what was actually good.

# Seventeen

EVERY DAY at the meditation retreat follows the exact same routine, but my brain turns each day into something wildly different. On day five I decide that Vipassana is the greatest thing in the world, and that when I'm out, I'll need to share it with all the people I love. On day six, I'm so ready to leave that all I can do is fixate on how to get my phone and computer back and slink away without anyone noticing. My day six brain believes it understands it all already, everything they're trying to teach me, and I just want to be back in the world where I can go to a diner and eat eggs Benedict. By day eight, I absolutely hate meditating and everyone there. I hate my own brain. I just want to not be in my body, in this room, anywhere.

I feel like I'm in prison. I mean, I know I'm not in Folsom. I can leave any time I want, but the fact that I don't makes me wonder what I really have to return to.

I once read an article in *The New York Times* about a university student named Swe Win, who was thrown in a Myanmar jail in 1998 on charges of distributing subversive pamphlets. He served seven years in solitary confinement. For a while he dreamed of reading a

book or talking to friends, but found the torture this brought to be too unbearable.

"My mental pain kept growing," he said, "until it dawned on me that I would go mad if I continued to want things I could not get. Although this was a moment of utter hopelessness, it ended my delusional urges."

He fashioned his own method of meditation by doing a sort of mental X-ray of his body, seeing it as a collection of bones radiating peace out to the world. After being released on amnesty, he went to a full Vipassana course to learn the proper method. Now he volunteers for a group that goes back into the same prison he was locked up in and teaches the prisoners the way I'm being taught right now.

But I don't feel like I'm doing this right. I have to stop letting my mind drift so far away. The more I think about all the times that are gone forever, the worse I feel. I can make my heart beat faster just by letting my mind slip into the past, but that doesn't change where I am, in the prison of the present tense.

Dear __________,

I don't want to say that I had a dream about you last night. A dream where you wouldn't talk to me, even though I kept passing by you, your neck always turned away from me, like you were avoiding a mosquito.

I don't want to say that there is a place I remember in a frozen attic somewhere in your hometown that I wish I could return to. Not that I particularly enjoyed the freezing or the lack of electricity, nor the old nudie magazines on the floor, nor the horrible state of the house, how the door wouldn't close because the extension cord went through the doorway and up to the attic to power a lamp. Just the way that it was so cold that it made sense to go to sleep naked with our bodies pressing together, as though we were in some Jack London survival scenario where our own heat was the only thing that could save us. I don't want to say that I think fondly of desperate situations, like when the battery in the van died and we had to wait around an extra hour with nothing to do. Or when we were in that town where they film the vampire movies and our cellphones didn't work and we had one bottle of Chardonnay to share in the back of my van.

I don't want to say that killing time with you is preferable to any kind of time with anyone else. I don't want to say that it's understandable if you do something awful because you're just so goddamned brilliant at it. I don't want to say that the way you broke me in half was art and that I should be praising you in galleries instead of cursing you while half-asleep alone in my van.

I don't want to say that a dream about you is still worthwhile even if you keep turning your neck away from me. I don't want to say that I wish I could call the you from a year ago, as there is no number for that person any more. There is no satellite that can beam a signal far enough to reach that version of you.

I don't want to say that I took two photos of you when I was pretending to look at my phone. One was at the Mexican restaurant when you were deciding what to order and you tucked your hair behind your ear. The other was of you putting on your clothes in that freezing attic. Both of those photos look blurred and obscene, like I was trying to capture a Sasquatch that I knew wouldn't stick around for long. I think because I stole those pictures I get no satisfaction in looking at them. It's like looking at a candle in the store wrapped in cellophane, when what I really want to see is the candle lit and glowing on an attic floor, wax dripping down and pooling on a saucer, two bodies sharing one sleeping bag, trying to keep warm, getting there.

We'll just leave those things unsaid,
Nick

# *Things for which we have no words*

1. If you plotted all the points of what has been the center of the known universe at different times throughout history—the town square, the middle of the earth, the sun, the galactic center—and drew a line between all those points, what would you call that line?

2. When you're sharing a treat with another person—let's say a cookie—and you get down to a little crumb, and one of you takes half of the crumb to leave a bite for the other person, and the other person takes half of the half of the crumb, what do you call that moment when you decide that it's ridiculous to keep halving this crumb, so you just pop the last bit in your mouth, but before you've even swallowed it you see this slight look of disappointment on the other person's face and you return the crumb to the tip of your tongue and just point at it and raise your eyebrow as if to say, "It's not too late—" and they turn away disgustedly. The feeling you have as you swallow that disputed crumb in your tight, guilty throat.

3. If you gathered together all the unpopped popcorn kernels from a batch and talked to them, I mean *really* talked to them and asked them why they didn't pop, what would you call that? *What's going on,*

*guys? Was it something I did? Did I put too much pressure on you?* Which would be the same word as the feeling of wanting someone to participate in a group event and putting all the elements in place just so, and having them decline for one reason or another—maybe a very good reason—but you don't really know because they're just sitting there not participating.

4. The sounds that appliances make that are not just the regular clicks and whirs of their everyday functions, the sounds that only happen when you haven't used or even considered the reality of that particular appliance in days. When suddenly there's a pause in the conversation or the music or the TV show and you stare at the wall with unfocused eyes and your appliance seems to let loose a sigh, as though it's trying to remind you what a burden it is, always being at your service, and it just wants to remind you, *Hey I'm a person too*, and you have about three-fourths of a second where you feel bad for it, as though it were your long-suffering butler with rheumatoid arthritis sighing because it's another Christmas that he spends away from his children, but then you catch yourself and think, *Wait, I'm feeling sorry for my fucking oven or whatever,* and you realize that you spent three-fourths of a second fully accepting the humanity of a machine that was assembled out of metal and glass and you feel a little embarrassed but also a little heartened that you have such an elastic sense of what's deserving of human dignity. The word for that feeling.

5. What do we call the spaces between the lines on a ruler that mark off the fractions of an inch? The width of the line has to be wide enough for you to be able to see it, but that width also makes it less accurate because you have to decide whether the fraction of an inch ends at the edge of the line or right in the middle, and then what is the width of the line itself and with what sort of ruler would we measure that width? There's the same question with time, because the ticks of a clock have a certain, or should I say uncertain, duration. Does the second begin on the "t" or on the "k" of "tick?" Don't forget

that the second hand must be moving slower at the beginning of the second than at the end, because it has to gain momentum and then it has to stop again, and do they calculate all of that when they're making one of those black-and-white round clocks that go in every classroom in every school? Because every second matters in school, it's almost terrifying to think of this finite amount of seconds and so much to learn, so we need to figure out the details of every corner of every second, but as soon as we isolate and try to savor the rear third of a second, for example, the hand has already ticked and tocked its way further down the road. So what are we counting, and what is uncountable? The word for what is uncountable.

6. The permanence of impermanent objects. A river is a constantly changing collection of water, but we signify it on the map with a solid blue line. The sky is always the sky no matter if it's red at dawn or purple at dusk or almost white at noon. The word for something

that is itself no matter how much you add or take away from it. The ocean. A mountain. You. What do we call that?

7. The word that every animal is really saying when it makes its cluck or whinny. It's something like, "Hey, I'm here, don't come over here," but it's mixed with, "I exist *too*, you know," and it also has a bit of, "Well, don't come over here, but at least *look* at me," and then some of, "Okay, come over here. I need to have your presence in front of me to define who I am." That word. It has to be short and guttural and it needs to be uttered without nuance or texture so that it can carry over fields and rattle under bridges and still be understood. Of course if there's only one word in your lexicon, there are probably unlimited variations of how you might pronounce it, but it's not like ducks are sitting around quacking and then they all stop and look at one that's doing it a little weird and give this sort of disgusted look like, "What did you just say? Did you say ... *quock?*" And the one duck in question is all like, "No, I said *quack*, just like you guys. Heavens."

8. Waking up from a really thorough dream, a dream so complicated and believable that it includes multiple acts and plot twists. A dream so deep that you have forgotten your non-dreaming identity—where you live, what you do for money, who you love—and so when you wake you need a good half hour to accept that you're you again. A dream so convincing that in only eight hours it erases thirty-plus years of evidence as to the permanence of your character and your essential circumstances, so that you need to adjust to being you again, and if anyone calls or comes in your room in that time period you have to tell them that you need more time to remember yourself. That period of time, particularly the start of it, where you're not entirely convinced that you are who you have been, or who you should be. The opportunity for reinvention that occurred effortlessly while you slept. The word for that.

9. The person you don't want to dream about but you can't stop dreaming about.

10. The word for a love letter that you wrote then erased, not just by deleting the email, but by going through the letter backwards word by word, erasing them one at a time while still hoping to find something that looks acceptable, that doesn't feel forced and wrong. Doing this every day, writing out letters in your head, thinking you've got them just right, then typing them up in the evening with everything feeling so wrong, and then deleting every word before bedtime, leaving just the word "Dear" at the beginning, thinking there can't be anything wrong with "Dear," and then ultimately deleting that too. If there's a word for that act of composing and then decomposing letters, write that word to me in an email, but before you send it, erase the word and delete the email and don't tell me about it.

# *Eighteen*

NEXT TO ME, the fidgeter is still swishing around every minute. I know it's ridiculous to feel competitive about this, yet I keep getting caught in an eddy of thought about how everyone around me is probably doing the meditation better than I am. As much as I've heard Goenka talk about how my reaction to a problem is worse than the problem itself, I sit here frustrated and mad. No amount of passive aggressive sighing or throat clearing is going to help.

I'm desperate to think about something—anything—else. Something silent. Like clouds. Clouds are like an enormous species of graceful, legless white buffalo that migrate above the world. They're like a family of acrobats, tossing each other across the sky, catching each other softly, changing shape with each embrace. They're always on the move, and they always move in complete silence, day and night. Creeping armies of clouds are sliding overhead right now as you suck on your milkshake, and you don't even hear them. What beast or machine or collective of organisms has ever moved such a great distance with such minimal audio output? Jesus, what *are* clouds?

*Shhhhhfffff.* The windbreaker pulls me back to earth.

Dear __________,

I wish I could live in Central Park. I would sleep in the center of the tulip garden, or under one of the bridges near the zoo. The custodians would tuck me in at night in my big cedar bed with five layers of thin blankets. I'd listen to the coyotes howl and the cicadas buzz and the lightning bugs flicker in the night air. I'd sleep that solid outdoor sleep, when your dreams connect with the roots and grow into the ground. I'd wake up right at dawn, when the garbage trucks start clattering and the city tries to rouse itself. I'd hide my bed under some bushes and sit on one of the big boulders overlooking the pond and read a book to myself. It would be so comforting to be in nature and yet be nestled in one of the busiest cities in the world, like being a kid and camping out in your own backyard, far enough outside that you could look at the stars but close enough that you could hear the din of the TV show your mom was watching, the laughter of the studio audience sometimes spilling over loud enough for you to catch it.

All I ever wanted was to run away and have someone chase after me.

Someday a book will be written about all of us. It will contain all of our arcs. Every betrayal, every coincidence. It will all line up, in this book. When we can read the whole story, all at once, it will all make so much sense. It will be years later and we'll all have figured out our loves by then, so we can laugh at the silly things we did that we thought were noble, and the noble things we did that we thought were terrible, and the terrible things we did that we thought were silly. We'll close the cover and put it away and laugh the knowing laugh that comes from recognizing how out of control of our own worlds we were.

Yours in pursuit of all of that,
Nick

# *Nineteen*

Paul Simon is onstage in Central Park. It is his reunion concert with Art Garfunkel on September 19th, 1981. Art has left the stage for a moment so that Paul can play a few songs on his own. One song in particular begins with just Paul on guitar. After the full-band songs that made up the first part of the concert, he is concerned with being heard over the din of the approximately half million people in attendance.

"Well I hope you can hear me, I'd like to sing a new song," he says. "I've recorded this song, and I've never performed it before, so this is the first time."

"The Late Great Johnny Ace" would appear on his 1983 album *Hearts and Bones* as the last track before a one-minute instrumental coda by Philip Glass. The album would be another disappointing commercial release for Paul Simon's solo career, and the last album before the wild multi-platinum success of *Graceland.*

In the weeks leading up to the concert, he felt insecure about performing at the behest of the Central Park Conservancy. He didn't think enough people would show up to raise money to help restore the park, which, like his career, was slowly deteriorating.

The song is about the R&B singer from the 1950s by the name of Johnny Ace, who had the bad habit of waving a gun around backstage at shows. One night in Houston he was doing just that and someone told him to be careful. Ace said, "It's alright, it's not even loaded!" He put the gun to his head to demonstrate and pulled the trigger. He was wrong.

Paul was very willing to play unreleased or unfinished songs during this part of his career. He once played a half-finished "Still Crazy After All These Years" on *The Dick Cavett Show*, pointing out that he was stuck on where to go for the bridge. It's hard to imagine a musician playing a half-finished song on national television today.

As he starts to play "The Late Great Johnny Ace" onstage in Central Park, the crowd continues to murmur, and Paul looks around somewhat uneasily. By the third verse of the song, the subject of the lyrics changes from the death of Johnny Ace to the death of John Lennon, which occurred less than a year ago, just a few blocks away.

Certainly the audience can feel the poignancy of this man, a contemporary of Lennon's, singing about this murder so close in time and space to the terrible event. About three and a half minutes into the song, Paul's voice rises at the apex of the line about staying out late at a bar with a stranger after hearing the news.

And right then, at the dramatic height of the song, a strange man bursts onstage. The video from the HBO feed of the event gets wavy, almost as though a poltergeist were interrupting the broadcast signal. The man closes in on Paul but is instantly grabbed by a stagehand and pulled away. The man is shouting, "I gotta talk to you. I gotta talk to you. I gotta talk to you."

Paul lets the last chord ring out as he backs off the mic and looks at the man. His low guitar string buzzes and begins to feedback a little. Then he pauses for an extended fermata, still musical in its timing, not interrupting the flow of the song, and finishes the last line.

The song ends with a solo guitar figure that goes on for about thirty seconds. As he plays it, Paul has the most fascinating look on his face. I've watched the video dozens of times and still can't quite read the complex expression of relief, fear, composure, and confusion. He must have felt at least momentarily that he would end up with the same fate as John Lennon.

Their lives had intersected before. Paul Simon and John Lennon took the stage together to present the Record of the Year at the seventeenth Grammy Awards in 1976.

They were inexplicably joined by the singer Andy Williams. In the tradition of awards shows, all three men were obliged to read corny scripted banter off of cue cards.

Lennon says, "Hello, I'm John. I used to play with my partner Paul."

Simon says, "I'm Paul, I used to play with my partner Art."

And Williams says, "I'm Andy, I used to play with my partner Claudine," which gets a big laugh and I'm not sure I really understand why. Andy leaves the stage after a couple more jokes, leaving just John and Paul at the podium. John is wearing a beret and a medal around his neck and seems to take none of it seriously. Paul is in a suit and stands a full head shorter than John. It is reassuring just to see them standing together, with the camera cutting to Yoko Ono sitting in the front row smiling and laughing. It is a warm night indoors in Southern California in the seventies and all the famous people are friends with each other.

The award for Record of the Year goes to Olivia Newton-John for "I Honestly Love You." The announcer says, "Accepting the award for Olivia Newton-John is ... Art Garfunkel!" and Art walks up to the stage wearing a long-sleeved black shirt with a painted-on tuxedo. When Art arrives at the podium, Paul tentatively shakes his hand and jokingly admonishes him, "I thought I told you to wait in the car."

A year after the Central Park concert, Paul was on *Late Night with David Letterman*. Letterman asks, "Do you ever worry for your own safety on stage?"

"No," Paul says. "I consider it. I consider it. I always consider it. And of course after John Lennon's murder, you have a heightened awareness of it. My reaction when that guy came up onstage was, I said, 'Ah, he's messed up the song.' It's a new song, I thought, it's hard enough for anybody to grasp a new song, especially if I'm singing it with just a guitar. Now this guy's come and he's messed up the song. My reaction at the time was not one of fear, and neither was Art's reaction, and he was sitting on the stage. I think what happened was—when we used to perform together, people would come up onstage all the time, but they were always bringing flowers or things. It was really a different time. We didn't have a sense of fear. You thought people could be a little bit crazy, but generally crazy in a benign way, and as it happens, this guy was also. He was stoned, he kept saying, 'Paul, I gotta talk to you. I gotta talk to you.' He wasn't threatening, although it might have looked that way."

Letterman then asks him if he would play a song. The crowd cheers as Paul looks around bashfully, seemingly surprised by the request. A stagehand brings out a guitar that Paul points out isn't his own.

He tries to stand for a second with the guitar, realizes it isn't right for the cameras and the lighting, then sits in an armchair. The arms, of course, make it really awkward for him to hold the guitar. Paul says he'll play the Johnny Ace song and the lights go down and a spotlight comes up. When he approaches the same part of the song that mentions John Lennon, he stops playing and looks quizzically at the guitar. The high E string has somehow gotten snagged on the neck, producing a muted, high, out-of-tune note. As soon as he stops, the crowd reflexively claps and the show cuts to a commercial. When they get back from the break, Paul explains what happened and says, "I'm now beginning to have my doubts about whether I should perform this song at all." Regardless, he finishes the song.

DEAR __________,

THERE IS A BELL in Oxford, England that has been ringing for 170 years. If one strike of a bell can have such long-lasting effects, if one quick action can outlive any human, then surely I can be struck emotionally by you and have it last a long time, long past the point where it's still understandable or relatable or even appropriate. It's not just something that I can shake off or forget. The bell is still ringing, vibrating, even if it's inaudible at this point. Sometimes I wish I could put my hand on the bell and stop the ringing, but mostly I'm glad to have been struck at all.

Yours, trembling,
Nick

# *Twenty*

The first time I went to New York City, I took the Greyhound from California. The three-day trip resembled the kind of waiting period they have for guns or marriage. *Are you sure you know what you're getting into?* I obsessed about the city as I rode through the cornfields of the Great Plains. I worried that everything in New York would be on fire, that the buildings would be jutting out at impossible angles, always about to fall on me.

Many years later I found myself spending a winter in a narrow apartment in Greenpoint with hissing steam heat. I had been assigned by my producer Kevin to write a song cycle about a citizen astronaut. Kevin stumbled upon the story after his second whiskey and coke on a transcontinental flight. Looking down at the clouds, he'd been wondering about his compatriots in hypoxia, the euphoric lack of oxygen to the brain one gets at high altitudes. And here, in a 1966 issue of *Life Magazine* he'd found online, was the story of Nick Piantanida.

Nick had been a truck driver, and before that a professional basketball player. He could've been a star for the Knicks if he had wanted, but instead he chose adventure. He went to South America to climb waterfalls. He wrestled cobras in bars. He was the man you turned to when things went wrong. If somebody burst through the doors of a restaurant with a gun, he was the man who would somehow handle everything.

"I thought he was Superman," his wife Janice said. "I didn't think anything could hurt him." Imagine getting to be the wife of Superman. At first you wouldn't believe that his gaze was genuine. You wouldn't be able to understand why he singled you out as the one he wanted to marry, why he'd slowly drive alongside you as you walked home, asking you over and over again for a date until you finally relented.

One early winter day, before the cold really set in, I took the ferry up the East River with Bonnie. She'd brought along a book of Emerson. We leaned over the railing and took pictures of ourselves in front of the New York skyline. "Every word was once a poem," she read aloud. I had met her over the summer, when I was in Denver on tour. Stelth had given copies of my album to everyone he knew, so that when I went through town all these people had heard my music. Bonnie was playing with her kids in a little wading pool and the water had gotten all over her dress. "I love your music," she said. And then, referring to her dress, "I'm sorry." "Yeah," Stelth said, "I'm sorry I love your music too." That night Bonnie invited me to play a show with her, and before I knew it, we were singing "Cincinnati" as a duet as though we had been singing it for decades.

That night in New York we went to the ballet, where we saw a Nico Muhly piece. A woman sang an Irish folk melody while the orchestra pulled against our expectations of what the harmonic structure would be. We sat up in the fourth balcony of that jewel box theater looking almost directly down on the performers. To us, the dancers looked like lovers. We leaned over the railing and once again took pictures of ourselves.

Like alcohol, New York is dangerous because it can make everything you do seem more important than it is. Often I'll think I've had an epic day there, but when I try to describe it to someone it ends up sounding like, "I went across town and had a bagel sandwich, and then I stumbled upon that shoe repair shop with the old man, but I didn't have the right pair of shoes with me, and then fortunately I managed to not get on the wrong train, and I figured out how to get back home avoiding those shuttle buses they have in Queens." Which is nothing. It's not a day at all, but in New York it feels almost legendary.

When I am staring over a cliff, afraid to jump, I think of certain magical people, like Nick Piantanida, and try to just do what they would do. Bonnie and Stelth, too—they'd jump off the cliff just like that, without hesitation. Unlike me, they don't let their minds spin out of control until they're awash with all the negative possibilities. Those two jump in the time it takes me to look down and consider the scene.

"When you were with Nick you didn't really need entertainment," Janice Piantanida said about her husband. "We were our own entertainment." Their song was the Acker Bilk clarinet instrumental "Stranger on the Shore," which they'd slow dance to in the local bar.

On another dry day, I walked through Central Park with Bonnie. Every time I go to that park I find something I've never seen before. I looked at her standing on a rock in front of the pond and I tried to make that moment permanent.

Nick Piantanida made the decision to go up in a gondola to over 120,000 feet, past the highest mark that Joseph Kittinger had ever reached, and jump out with a parachute and float to the ground. This was in the mid-sixties, before the United States had sent a man to the moon. Going up in space still required miles of faith as well as big-time technological know-how. There was still so much that had never been done before. Science and mathematics can help with pinning down ideas of how objects and bodies will behave in different environments, but there is still the cold reality of the moment, when a parachute is supposed to open up in the stratosphere, and the few yards of carefully manufactured fabric will either behave like people expect it to or not.

That winter, there was a big snowstorm that hugged the city. They closed all the schools, a rarity for New York. It seemed like all the kids and teachers in the city had come to the park to sled down the hills. I took video of them falling on their backs and laughing, of the gnarled snowmen they made, of me wiping snow off the statues of Shakespeare and Columbus as though I were discovering forgotten heroes in some long-distant future. Then I put my camera away and got in line to ride a sled.

My favorite art connects two different things and shows how they are related. When I was stuck in a fearful marriage, living in a dark basement in Portland, infected with ringworm and pulling out my hair, I wrote a song comparing my life to the Siege of Leningrad, which happened during World War II, when the Nazis surrounded the Russian city for nine hundred days and slowly starved the citizenry.

> Some of the shame that we still carry
> Is from falling in love and oh we feel embarrassed
> Because so many people didn't make it
> out of the city that year

Maybe it's disrespectful to compare widespread starvation to an unhappy marriage, but it's no different than comparing a band of metal to the sound of a bell. A ring is *like* this. It could never *be* this. There are echoes of one in the other.

I sat in that apartment in Greenpoint writing a song cycle about Nick Piantanida. The steam hissed through the pipes like air leaking out of an oxygen mask. I didn't even really know what a song cycle was when Kevin asked me to do it. Kevin had written an epic poem that was to form the basis of the lyrics, but it was hard to graft those words to music and keep them all up in the air. I laid out the sheets of the poem on the carpet and circled above them as if I were descending in a parachute, trying to find a place to land. It is always this way with songs. Words are like lead weights holding down the balloon of music, and most of the work involves setting the balance. Of course when you're writing a song cycle about an actual balloon trip, it's twice as important not to have the words scuttle everything.

Greenpoint is the old Polish part of Brooklyn, which means that there are old Polish people shuffling down the sidewalks in heavy coats. Everyone in the Associated Supermarket on Manhattan Avenue speaks Polish and the old ladies ask if you can reach the pickled herring off the top shelf for them. I am half Polish, from my father's side. When I was a kid the first person whose music really reached me was Chopin. His "Prelude in E minor" was a shot right to my stomach. Some music you struggle to appreciate, and some just tackles you and tramples your heart. Before I ever knew how to play an instrument I used to have dreams of being able to play the piano like Chopin. In my dreams I would look down at my hands and marvel at what they could do. My left hand would stretch to pound out strong octaves in the bass line. My right hand would hit minor seventh chords and let in just enough of that breath that acknowledges the struggle of life. A few years later, a psychic told me that in a past life I had been a woman living in Poland in the nineteenth century and that I had taken piano lessons from Chopin. She had no idea what Chopin meant to me.

Kevin, Nathan, and I went to Union City, New Jersey, hoping to find some remains of Nick Piantanida's story. The town itself seemed impossibly run-down considering it was just a few miles from all the thrilling potential of Manhattan. All the old bars had new names. Inside were no memories of the man. The only tangible sign of Nick was in the cemetery outside of town, where we found his tombstone amongst the thousands there on a hill overlooking the high rises of the big city. His epitaph was from a Walt Whitman poem:

> I am an acme of things accomplished
> and an encloser of things to be

Once in a while I'll convince myself that every song has been written. After all, there are only twelve notes to choose from. There are a finite number of chords, tempos, and rhythms. We've all just been repeating what has already happened.

That is looking at it backwards, though. A song does not happen because you pick chords and a melody and then put words to it. A song is born from an emotion or a state of being, a person standing somewhere and describing a perspective that only they can see. This energy is then harnessed into the structure of a song. Complexity or innovation in determining which chords go where is valuable, but if done for its own sake it is missing the point. You could write a song with fifty-nine chords that says nothing. On the other hand, you could write a song that is one chord, a melody that is one note, lyrics that are one word, and if you do so with genuine intent and sincere emotion, you could say everything.

I've always thought that folk music is defined by its insistence on telling the stories of people who don't have a voice because they are either poor, oppressed, or dead. The story of Nick Piantanida is a folk tale.

The music I looked to for inspiration was Bach, whose non-dynamic cascades of notes sounded to me like a pedal-powered balloon floating in the air. When I was young I never really responded emotionally to Bach. He wasn't as romantic as Chopin, and for a time, his music reminded me of a math equation. My appreciation for him started to blossom when I realized that every cellist can play his "Cello Suite in C" from memory, and are generally happy to do so upon request, even if you catch them walking through the subway on their way to rehearsal. Eventually I learned that during Bach's life, keyboards had no dynamics. He was just working with the tools he had. The mathematical structures he built have become as beautiful to me as slowly-opening hyacinths. Their complexity is, in fact, what makes them emotional.

Nick Piantanida made three ascents. The first time up, fierce winds shredded the balloon to pieces. The second time up, Nick couldn't release himself from the gondola due to a valve on the oxygen line that was supposed to detach but had become stuck. He rose up to the desired height of 120,000 feet but was unable to jump out, no matter how much he thrashed at the line with his puffy gloved hands. So he sat in the basket as it went all the way back down to Earth, a humiliating and nauseating descent for such an experienced skydiver.

On the third ascent, Nick's facemask cracked. He was already above 50,000 feet, far too high to be able to breath enough oxygen. He experienced that euphoric state of hypoxia and on his way back to earth went brain dead. Four months later, he died. He left behind a wife and two children. "I thought he was Superman. I didn't think anything could hurt him."

Kevin decided to put the song cycle in between two ballets on a program of music. He thought that since ballet is about the struggle of trying to escape the tie of gravity, it would be revelatory to the audience if there were a piece in the middle that had no constraints. To that end, we hired a choir to sing the piece, thinking that from the lowest note of a male bass to the highest of a female soprano there is a range equal to that of the height of the Earth's atmosphere. It didn't work. Though the voices did express a certain kind of freedom, the audience was just watching a bunch of singers standing there onstage, a pretty boring thing to watch immediately after some of the best athletes in the world had danced for the previous half hour.

When we premiered the program in New York, the whole piece was sung by my friend Kaylee. Her voice has a great weight to it, which is, ironically, precisely what the piece needed. It still didn't make much of an impression on a crowd that had come to watch ballets.

I was greeting people after the show, standing on the shiny marley flooring, when I dropped a quarter. It rolled over to Bonnie's feet. "Did you drop something?" she asked. We went for a drink in Hell's Kitchen, and she told me how much she liked the very end of the song cycle, a piece called "Partition" that features a heartbreaking piano figure composed by my friend Edward. I told her it represented the moment when Nick Piantanida's brain dies, when he finally finds peace while looking out at the beauty of the curved horizon. She asked me to repeat the lines.

> Your face is softter
> than the curvature of Earth
> you see I'm only
> away for a while
> I have gone collecting

All his planning for the big launch had been with one distinct vision in mind: that he would end up on the ground and kiss his wife and know that he was the first man to do this amazing thing. The fact that he never physically made it to the parade doesn't matter. In his mind, in those last moments he stepped from the gondola right into the backseat of a car driving down the main street of Union City. He began to smile and wave at his adoring friends, and never stopped.

# *Twenty-one*

When I fell in love with Melanie I started going to church for the first time in my life. She was Christian and I had no particular grievance against Christianity from childhood so I went to see what I could learn. The church was progressive and non-denominational. The pastor dressed in jeans and a turtleneck and told us about the Book of Matthew. In it, Jesus gives his sermon on the mount and says to the gathered crowds, "You are the salt of the earth. But if the salt loses its saltiness, how can it be made salty again?" The pastor said that we needed to remember that whenever men talk, they are distracted by their own biases and interests. The only way you can be sure you're getting the truth is to get the word directly from God.

It made me think of my own biases, and how confusing it can be to find the truth amongst mortals filled with fears and desires. And then it occurred to me that although he was a pastor, he was still just a man. The words he was reading were written down by men. Even if they had originally been spoken by God, someone had to remember them and write them down. I know that any time I've been interviewed for a newspaper article, even when the person takes notes and uses a recording device, something always gets jumbled.

In my case, just a musician promoting an album, it's no big deal if some words are mixed up. But if I were laying out the tenets of a religion, I'm not sure I'd feel comfortable relying on the accounts of earwitnesses.

As a metaphor, the Bible meant a lot to me. You could even say that it changed my life in that it helped me to see the humbling power of the universe. But as long as I only saw it as a metaphor, my appreciation of it gave me no currency with Christians. They knew that I didn't feel the same way. They were right. I didn't.

On Easter Sunday one year, Melanie had just returned from Los Angeles, where she'd spent several months working as a camera assistant on a television show. When she left I wrote her an email telling her how I felt, and she wrote back telling me she felt the same way. But now that we were back in the same physical location, it wasn't so easy to know what to do, perhaps because the first time we saw each other after the email exchange was at church. Everyone remembers about Jesus around the holidays, so the room was packed. One of the ushers told me that there were empty seats in the balcony, but I smiled and pointed at my friends. Lori let me squeeze by because she had anxiety if she couldn't sit next to the aisle.

I touched Melanie's head and she grabbed my arm, the only kind of hug you can possibly do in a crowded church pew. The band launched into a song. It went, "He is risen. Hallelujah." The violinist had some trouble with his microphone, which was giving off a hum. Melanie leaned in and asked me, "What is that sound? Is that feedback?" and I said, "No. That's the Holy Ghost. He has come back." She laughed and blushed. A small victory.

The pastor spoke about the infinite Jesus. Forever has he loved us and forever will he love us. A Jesus for every moment in the history of the universe. A long row of them, stretching out as far as you could hope to see. Melanie's arm leaned against mine. I tried to think of a question to ask her. I wanted another opportunity to lean in towards her, another chance to make her laugh, to see her smile. All I could think of were all those Jesuses.

The service ended and we walked outside into the rain. Melanie and Lori drove to the store to get honeyed ham and shortbread and strawberries for brunch. I got in my own car and returned to the old house where I once lived with Amanda. Everyone was in the kitchen while I stayed in the living room, playing the piano. Melanie wore a small green lacy apron around her waist and looked like a ballerina. I played the holiest songs I knew, trying to reach her. "Pyramid Song." "The Chalet Lines." "Jealous Guy." "Hallelujah."

With every new chord progression, I tortured myself a little more over the missed opportunities, like that night I'd seen her in the hallway in her muumuu. Why did that moment end so suddenly? Why didn't I steal just a few more seconds to look at her? Why do moments like that go by so quickly when Easter Sunday lasted on and on?

Melanie and Lori finished preparing Easter brunch and set it out on the table. Amanda was there, as was the crazy Greek roommate, and the lesbian roommates who loved watching "Law & Order" and ordering Domino's pizza. I sat at the head of the table and carved the ham. I didn't live there anymore, but everyone looked at me to say grace. We all held hands. On one side of me was Amanda, on the other side the Greek girl, who held Melanie's hand. I stumbled through something along these lines: "This strange group of people have all managed to find themselves here at this table today. May each one of us endure, as Jesus has endured, for on this day he rose from the grave. God bless the food we are to eat. Amen." I wish I'd said something else, like, "I've seen your flag on the marble arch." I wish I would've been one seat closer to Melanie. I wish it would've been her hand in mine. "Love is not a victory march," I would have continued, and she would've slowly closed her eyes and smiled and blushed, bleeding through the cover of her book that so many people find so hard to read. "It's a cold and it's a broken Hallelujah," I would have concluded, and I would've liked to have seen what happened to Easter brunch then.

I once read that there are 313 exclamation points in the Bible. Even for a book of miracles that seems excessive. The book I want to write is a book documenting miracles. I'm not interested in the miracles of men, not even holy men. I want to tell you about miracles of nature, miracles of chance, how the sun is four hundred times bigger than the moon, but it's four hundred times further away, so it appears the same size in the sky. I think it's more miraculous to believe that it all came together naturally than to think that somebody made it with his big hands. I don't want big hands carving mountains and making giraffes. I want to marvel at the miracle of those things arising out of balls of dust.

After attending church with Melanie a dozen times, I wrote what I thought was a sincere song about what would happen if I truly accepted Jesus in my heart. The desire to make it poetic perhaps stretched it into something less than reverent.

> If I were to make things right with Jesus
> would he barely say a word
> like some drunken mynah bird?
> if I were to make things right with Jesus
> would he treat me like just another customer?

You can't get cute with songs about Jesus, though. Melanie made that clear in her reaction to the song. It's not enough just to mention Jesus, even if it's part of an honest struggle to understand. Either you're all in on the guy or you're not.

# Twenty-two

Even though Vipassana meditation was developed by the Buddha, it has no religious component. This is a large part of why I'm here: other than pledging not to speak or cause harm, I don't have to pretend to believe in anything. I'm allowed to take my own path in getting over annoyances like the man shuffling in his seat next to me. And even when I'm able to ignore the distractions of the man whose name I'll never know, I'll still have my own heartbreak to sit with. The beating of that drum is louder than all the swishing windbreakers in the world.

In the title track of *Graceland,* Paul Simon sings about a girl who comes back into his life, solely, it seems, to remind him that she's not there anymore. How it feels like a window in your heart with the wind blowing through. That window is what brought me to the retreat. I felt like I had wrapped my heart around someone that I loved and that that person, feeling frightened or suffocated by that love, had blasted her way out of my embrace with a shotgun, leaving a big hole in my heart through which the wind now blew.

Everybody walking by could look right through me and wave to people on the other side.

# *Twenty-three*

Can a song be a prison?

Years ago I saw Tom Waits play at the Paramount Theater in Seattle. The tickets cost ninety dollars, which was half of what I had in my bank account, but I never really considered not going. It was winter and I was driving an old pickup truck with no heat. I didn't know anyone in Seattle, so I had to drive up to the show and drive home after it, a round trip of six hours.

Somehow he played song after song that I didn't really want to hear. I kept thinking, "This song? Really?" Every goddamned song was like that. The band sounded great and it was nice to be in the same room as Tom Waits, but as the set was nearing its end I hadn't heard a song that killed me, which was strange because most of his songs kill me.

He finished the set without playing any songs on piano. There wasn't even a piano onstage. The crowd cheered for an encore and he came back out and played three more songs. Again, none of them were my favorites. This seemed like staggeringly long odds, that an artist I knew and loved so much would play so many songs I wasn't fond of. He finished the encore and the crowd cheered again and I sat there thinking, "I spent half of my savings on this and drove up here in a cold truck, and if he doesn't come out for a second encore, I'm going to have get back in that truck and drive three hours to Portland, where I have neither work nor money." Along with hundreds of others, I screamed for him to come back, wishing so hard that they would bring a piano out and he would play a song that I loved, knowing that at any second the house lights might come on and the show would be over.

Two stagehands wheeled out an upright piano and I started to cry. Tom Waits played "Hang Down Your Head" and I sang along with every word. I was fine with driving home three hours in the cold to a place where I had nothing. I was fine with everything. I got to hear one song I loved.

Years later when I met Rachel I found out that she was at that same show with her then-boyfriend. They weren't getting along and she spent most of the night arguing with him in the lobby of that beautiful theater.

On the day of my thirtieth birthday I was too sad to answer my phone so I drove out to the coast by myself. I wandered around until I discovered the Columbian Cafe in Astoria. I sat at the bar while Uriah, the owner, a very Jerry Garcia-looking man, cooked up different experiments. "Here, try this," he would say as he handed me a corn blini or a piece of roast duck dancing with flavor. I decided to order the red snapper, and he served it to me with a sliced-up tomato on top. I had never really enjoyed raw tomatoes. Not that I hated the taste, but for some reason they always made me gag. By the time I would finish a salad or something, my plate would be filled with little leftover tomato wedges that I had pushed aside. However, as Uriah handed me the plate of red snapper and tomato, despite thirty years of evidence to the contrary, I decided to eat it. I trusted his kind face and the loving way he cooked everything. I trusted the deep red of the tomato, the kind of red you only see when you cut a vein and blood comes spilling out.

I ate Uriah's tomato, and it changed everything. It made me mad at all the pale pink tomatoes that were, at that very moment, being shoved dispassionately into sandwiches and burritos. In the *Allegory of the Cave*, Plato describes how we never know the true essence of something, we just know the shadow that it casts on the wall of the cave in which we're all chained. I swear to God that in Astoria on my birthday when I bit into that tomato at the Columbian Cafe I walked right into that cave, grabbed the tomato that was casting the shadow of tomatoes all over the world and took a bite out of *that*.

It made me wonder how often in my life I had settled for the shadows. I wanted to find more real tomatoes.

I don't know how a song goes from just being a song to being "our song," a song you share with someone as a kind of lifelong secret. For me and Rachel that song was Waits' "All the World Is Green," but I can't remember how it became that. Ideally a song becomes "our song" in a magical moment when it comes on the jukebox and you just sort of naturally claim it together and it always reminds you of the other person. The only time anything so immediate has happened to me I was at Aunt Tiki's on Decatur with Leah and there was no one else there, so the bartender was playing the most punishing death metal imaginable at the loudest possible volume. We couldn't even have a conversation. It seemed ridiculous to just be sitting there holding our bottles of High Life, so during a merciful moment of silence I told her, "The next song that comes on is our song." Right then Dethklok's "I Ejaculate Fire" came on, and we almost fell off our barstools laughing.

That was just a joke, though. “All the World Is Green” was no joke. It was almost like a weapon, a way to remind each other how deep we had gotten, and if the other one ever shied away for even a moment it was a sharp reminder. “See? We are tied together.”

The first time I remember hearing it together we weren’t even together. We were at the same party, but it was inappropriate for me and her to be together, it being so uncomfortably close to her time with a good friend of mine. We had both made mistakes and were cowardly about it, so we decided to pretend not to know one another in public, which like pretending to work is one of the more exhausting and pointless things you can do with your time. At one point that night she left and she made it clear she wanted me to wait at the party for her.

I felt like I was caught in a film noir. I was falling in love with the wrong woman for the wrong reasons, but it never crossed my mind to walk away from that party. I waited for her in the living room with a guy whose name I never learned and who I wouldn’t recognize if he introduced himself to me right now. Tom Waits was on the CD player and that song came on. “Of course,” I thought, because the song seemed to sum up everything about me and Rachel. When it finished I went over to the stereo and hit repeat. I kept repeating it over and over again while I waited in that living room. Eventually I looked over at the guy and said, “Sorry, I need to keep hearing this song.” He was transfixed in his own way. “No,” he said. “It’s great.”

I was reminded of the old house on Emerson I lived in with Amanda, back when we were still married. We originally shared it with a bunch of painters. I’d come home late at night and Lesli would be painting. Painters are always trying to freeze a moment in time, and one time I came home and she had Jeff Buckley’s version of “Hallelujah” on repeat. This was before it was a popular song to cover for singing competitions, if you can imagine such a time. I sat down on the couch and heard "Hallelujah" over and over again and couldn't move because it pinned me down. I had never in my life listened to a song more than once in a row, I had never even considered the possibility, but for Lesli it was basically a part of the painting process.

It doesn't matter how many times I listened to "All the World Is Green" in that living room, waiting for Rachel to return. Fifteen, twenty, fifty—when she came back things were never the same. We ended up walking all the way from Northwest to Southeast Portland as the sun rose. Her eyes dulled as the night wore off. The world was getting darker, all her optimism seeping out just as the sun was coming up. On the Burnside Bridge she started to panic. Everything was falling apart in her mind and all I could think to do was remind her that it was just chemicals in her brain.

No matter if we were escaping a party in her '61 Valiant or we were walking on opposite sides of the reflecting pool in front of the Lincoln Memorial, all the world was green. The song always came up on a mix, or an iPod on shuffle, or just in our heads, always at the perfect moment. The two of us always dressed in black, as though we were in mourning for the mistakes that we made. Even when we were in Buenos Aires in the summertime, it was always black. One day when we were there we ducked into an old church where a choir was singing songs that echoed in the rafters. The plaster was in disrepair and falling down in white flakes. Every few seconds another tiny piece would fall on us. And each time, we would turn to each other with a look of, "Are you crying?" "No, just plaster. Are you crying?" "Plaster." Piece by piece this wonderful church in San Telmo was crumbling. How much can a ceiling fall apart until you can't live under it anymore? We stayed for one more song and then walked out, brushing the dust off our clothes.

One day Rachel showed me a new tattoo she had gotten on her arm of an anchor and some waves. She said it was partly because she was born in Anchorage, but it was also because of the line in that song that I had quoted to her once: "Marie, you are the wild blue sea." This was who she was, she told me, the wild blue sea. I didn't say anything, but I realized that I had misquoted the words to her, the actual phrase being "wild blue sky."

As soon as people started picking unripe tomatoes and shipping them far away, they should've been called something else, but it's hard to send back your plate of shadows and ask for real tomatoes. A large part of my struggle with Rachel was that I was the first man to ever really say no to her. If I were as beautiful and vibrant as she was, I too would have believed that I never needed to spend a night alone if I didn't want to. I admire that confidence. It's the only way to really get what you want in the world.

After Rachel and I finally split, any time I would hang out with a woman, I found myself missing our struggle. At dinner I'd keep waiting for the one word I'd say that would lead to the big argument. It never came. We would just eat our Pad Thai and then go watch a movie. Maybe the women I met after Rachel were afraid to push me because they didn't want to push me away. Or they didn't feel they deserved the absolute best that the world had to offer. Maybe they were just content to have normal, quiet evenings. On those evenings I felt like we were just making shadow puppets, content to recognize shapes that represented things we'd heard about.

Years later, after Rachel had moved to Australia and gotten married, she asked me if I would play a show for her when she was back in Portland at the end of the summer. She said she'd really love to listen to me in a quiet space, so I set up a show at a small bar called Savoy. As it turned out, this was the only time all her friends were in one place, catching up, which meant it was a night of people talking through my entire set. It felt pointless. I had just played a dozen shows on tour in the Midwest to quiet respectful audiences and here in my hometown I was tearing up my voice trying to sing over the noise of the crowd. She talked and laughed with all her friends, who were also my friends, but were really her friends. I played "All the World Is Green" that night, but I honestly don't even know if she could hear me.

# *Twenty-four*

I WROTE A SONG for Rachel about the magic of her eyes and how they inspired so many feelings in me that seemed crazy and untenable, and that I so desperately wanted those feelings to be real. The chorus of that song, "Sebastopol," goes:

> Your eyes tell so many tales
> your eyes tell so many wild wild tales
> your eyes tell so many tales
> oh and I only want to believe

She understood that it was a love song, even though the feeling I was expressing was more like how you'd regard a beast whose back you were clinging to for fear of getting tossed aside. After we broke up, the song was another kind of tether between us as we slowly shifted our orbits.

I said that I wanted to believe. I didn't say that I could.

Proust wrote, "Sometimes we mobilize all our spiritual forces in a glittering array in order to bring our influence to bear on other human beings who, we very well know, are situated outside ourselves where we can never reach them."

I was helping a friend move across the country in a rented Penske truck (something I've done more than once) when the musicality of the name Cincinnati struck me. The beginning of my song "Cincinnati" goes:

> I've sung you all the songs that I know
> I've told you all the stories from the circus show
> I've shown you all the ways I've tried to die
> oh I'm in love with you and you know why

When I pictured eventually playing that song in the city of Cincinnati I imagined that it would be received by a joyous audience lifting me up on their shoulders and carrying me away. Or at least they would be charmed by it, as a city. They would collectively blush and cross their legs and say, "Who, ME?!" I figured an unassuming Midwest city probably doesn't get a lot of songs written about it.

When in actuality I found myself on a tour that stopped in Cincinnati, I played a show with my band in the back room of a church in Cincinnati's university district. The whole time onstage I felt like I had a bar of chocolate I was hiding from them, this special gift I would bestow, and a few songs into the set I told the very small audience that I had written a song about their town. I knew that it wasn't the right energy in the room, but there was no way I could control that. I knew I wouldn't be lifted up on anyone's shoulders. I played the song anyway, and there was some polite applause that sounded hollow in that large reverberant church. For the remainder of the show, I felt the sting of having cared too much about something that was inherently stupid to care about.

The day after the show I returned to the church with my string players Danah and Dorota. We spent an hour running through songs. The last notes of our rehearsal were hanging in the air with unbridled hope, like the first drops of morning dew materializing in the air, when a woman from the adjoining café opened the big folding doors. "You guys don't happen to have a black Honda Civic, do you?" she asked. Her tone did not imply that someone had done something wonderful to that Civic, like given it a bath and waxed it up really shiny. We said that we did in fact have a black Honda Civic and she led us out into the parking lot where we saw that an elderly woman had plowed her car into ours, collided with the side of a wall, hit three more cars, and then crashed through a brick garage. It was like looking at the path of a small tornado. My first thought when considering the insurance ramifications of such an event, not to mention our altered travel plans, was, *Well, this is going to be complicated.* My second thought was, *God DAMN it, Cincinnati.*

Writing a song about a place and then expecting some sort of reciprocation is obviously foolish, but is it any sillier than writing a song that tries to change a person's heart?

Part of the allure of becoming a songwriter, I think, is this idea that you can have an effect on people's emotions. A love song has the potential to be a sort of love potion, claiming a person's heart by showing them how much you love them and how beautifully you can state that love. The thing is, I've tried this approach with women and it hasn't worked. I've talked with other songwriters about this because I'm curious if it has ever worked for anyone. Some of them aren't as interested in the love potion aspect of songwriting. It's possible I am just operating with an outdated vision in my head of a linocut old-timey man in stockings and a puffy shirt holding a lute just so and sitting under a balcony playing a song for a woman with long, curly hair.

I asked my friend and fellow songwriter Dustin Hamman if he believes in the power of a song when wooing a particular person. He said no.

**DUSTIN:**

The guy who used to go under the balcony and play his lute just did it because he didn't have any shows to invite a girl to.

Whereas you have a valid platform to impress people already. You can play a show on a stage in a bar.

**ME:**

But it's not just about impressing someone. It's writing a song for a particular person, and hoping that the song can woo them and win their heart, and in my experience it has failed pretty miserably.

**DUSTIN:**

Well that's because that will never work. It's like saying, "I'm a magician and I'm in love with this girl and I pulled a rabbit out of my hat and she still wouldn't marry me. I don't understand it."

You write good songs, she already knows that. It's all the other shit that you fucked up.

Indeed, the problem doesn't come from not writing a good enough song. It comes from not being able to live up to the emotions of that song. Historically, I have been more interested in expressing extreme cinematic emotions than in passing the salt shaker. During our confusing, never-realized relationship, I wrote a song called "I Know I'm Your Man" for Melanie. Instead of pining for something I wasn't getting (which I had already done plenty of) I decided to write a song from an optimistic viewpoint. Melanie and I weren't together in any way, but the song I wrote came out of imagining what I would sing to her at our wedding, if we ever had one. It was a lie, but a lie with some delicious ironies I could marinate in every time I performed it.

It seems to me that the best love songs paint a kind of darkness before lighting a way through it, and so the song begins with these lines:

> I tell lies you see through
> you tie ties I undo
> I know birds don't fly
> in a figure eight
> you know I can't walk
> on a line so straight
> everybody knows the girl with wine-stained hands
> but I know I'm your man

When I sent the song to Melanie, her only response was, "I don't drink wine," which I thought was a tragic misinterpretation. The song didn't work for its intended purpose. And yet, over the years, many friends have asked me to sing it at their weddings. It's a bittersweet feeling to know that this song, which had no effect on the person I wrote it for, has ended up touching others, as though I am watching my arrow miss its target, then split into shards and hit some other poor folks.

Years later, I asked Melanie over bowls of oatmeal at a diner on SE Hawthorne in Portland what she really thought of that song.

**MELANIE:**

> I remember when you first sent me that song. I was in Nicaragua at an Internet café. It's obviously really magical and really beautiful.
>
> It did make me cry. But there's this essence too where there are moments where it starts to feel disingenuous. The actions weren't matching up with

the words. It feels self-serving, that you're just doing this for yourself. And it seems so pretty in this moment, and it is, it's gorgeous, but it feels cheapened by actions not being genuine.

**ME:**

Does it have any value to you, having a song written about you?

**MELANIE:**

It's beautiful, it's painful, it's complex, it's annoying. It makes me feel special. Everyone wants to feel special.

You were never really very good about telling me that those songs were about me. I think you wrote them to process your emotions in a cathartic way, and that I was a part of that, but you'd never really say they were about me. Only about a year ago did you start pointing out songs. I think you held that information hostage. You did it as a love note, but you didn't tell me.

In a way, each song is a conversation that you could've had with me, and they would've been great conversations, but instead you wrote a song. I think you go deeper with the emotions in your songs than you do in conversation. Or the songs come across that way, because I projected into them what the meaning was.

Which is a good point, but if we all were able to converse freely with everyone we were in love with and there were no stifled emotions or kinks in the hose it's likely that we wouldn't be left with any songs. Or perhaps we'd write rudderless songs of pure, calm emotion that just drift along without any interesting trouble to disturb them and give them shape. That is not to say that we need to create turmoil for the sake of making music, but rather that a certain difficulty in communicating emotions in conversation dovetails quite nicely with that moment when you sit down with your lute and start looking for a subject to sing about.

Most of the love songs I've written are about drowning in a lost love for someone, trying to find the edges of the body of water into which I've been hopelessly cast, such as in my song "I'll Become Everything." I was staying at a friend's house and he handed me an old classical guitar that had a rope instead of a strap and challenged me to write a song on it. I picked it up and went upstairs to a room in his house that was empty and therefore offered its own natural reverb. Sometimes trying to match the speed and tail of an echo can help dictate the tempo and purpose of a song. I wrote a song for Bonnie while in the middle of that twisting feeling of being miles and miles apart from having what I wanted.

I'll become  
I'll become  
everything that you want  
I'll become  
I'll become  
every signal, every spark  
I'll become  
I'll become  
all the swans in the park

I knew it was a desperate sentiment, but it felt true. I would love to write songs about my better moods, but they are often stuck behind dragons of longing, and I have to hack my way through those creatures to get to the open meadows. The finished songs are the carcasses of slain beasts I'm tossing aside as I work my way through.

Two years after writing that song I talked with Bonnie on the phone while she was driving through a carwash.

**ME:**

What is it like to have a song written about you?

**BONNIE:**

The only songs that I have ever known to have been about me have been the "I don't understand why it's not working out between us" kinds of songs. So I always think, "Oh no, we're miscommunicating and now it's become a song."

When I was sixteen my friend Chris wrote a song about me and it was a great emo song, and he actually said in it, "And if our eyes ever meet again, I'll be everything you thought I was." Because I just thought very highly of him and he wanted to be what I saw.

And then the song that we're speaking of is, "I'll become everything that you want." It's really funny because it seems to be a theme for me, these songs. It's never like, "You're the girl of my dreams," it's like, "What the hell is wrong here? This should be working out, and it's not."

Songs are born from a little bit of drama. It's taking something that was really personal and intimate between two people and making it public.

But it's still only one person's perspective. Maybe it would be different if a couple wrote a song as a duet to each other: "This is how I feel about you."

**ME:**

Would it be different if someone wrote a song and said, "I'm going to play this for you in person, I'm never going to record it, I'm never going to play it in public, it's just for you?"

**BONNIE:**

Wow. I feel like that would be more intimate than being lovers. Especially if you have a gift for music or poetry, and you wrote something for someone and you gave it to them as a gift in that way.

**ME:**

What is the value, to you, of having a song about you?

**BONNIE:**

If I was to die tomorrow and there was some sort of memory of me in the world and someone was like, "Oh that guy wrote a song about her that one time and it's super famous now—"

I mean, no, that would never happen. No one would say that. The songs take on their own life, it really doesn't have anything to do with me. Although it's a little bit flattering to think of myself as a muse.

I guess it means that we're not boring people. We're inspired and inspiring. So that's affirming.

**ME:**

But it's not any more personal than that?

**BONNIE:**

It's that you've recorded this beautiful interaction between two people, and that's what poetry is, the child of that interaction, but it doesn't necessarily mean that it will bond the two of you. It's unto itself. It's its own individual. In the same way, you can't have a child without two beings coming together—I mean test tubes and stuff, maybe, but normally you can't—and maybe it's the same with poetry. You can't have the poetry without these two beings having the interaction that they had, which produces that certain work of art. And so in

> a way you are connected forever through that. But maybe that's difficult to handle if you feel that that wasn't necessarily the reality for both of you at the time. It's like if someone froze sperm and then said, "This is your kid," and you said, "Hey, I didn't sign up for that. I don't know, is that my kid? Do I have any ownership over it whatsoever? Or is that your kid because *you* made it?"

The conversation was cut short when Bonnie had to pay for the car wash. It was becoming clear, though, that the songs I have written for people have not done anything to make them fall in love with me. If they were already in love, that love remained. If they weren't, the song wasn't going to make a difference. In fact, all that writing love songs has done is to make the subjects of those songs want *me* to change—or, rather, to want me to stop trying to change to make them happy. Instead of transforming myself into a swan to become something that a person could find beautiful, Bonnie's response was, "Who you are already is enough. Well, not enough for us to be together, but no amount of you changing is going to alter the situation between us."

Maybe it's a faulty male-centric Manifest Destiny sort of attitude that makes me think I can claim someone with my song and make them mine, even though the songs I write are, at least on the surface, vulnerable and tender and not likely to capture someone by force. I talked to my friend Laura about how she looks at love songs.

**LAURA:**

> I've been thinking about it. You're always writing these love songs and I think—

**ME:**

> You mean me?

**LAURA:**

Yeah, you, Nick Jaina. You write these love songs and I think, *I want to write a song like that, where I will lose myself for someone.* When I listen to love songs it's so powerful. Something about that makes the listener take these deep breaths and feel something. But I have the hardest time writing from that perspective and I don't know if it's because as a woman I've been taught all these feminist messages about being strong and not submitting yourself to another person, so there's a part of me that fights that, or feels it's impossible for me to even write a song whose message would be, "I love you so much that I'd lose myself for you," because there's that part of me that's like, "No. Hold on. You can't lose yourself."

I almost feel envious of all you male songwriters, because no one is going to doubt your strength or call you codependent or unhealthy. When a man writes a song like that it's beautiful, but when a woman does, it sounds like she's needy.

I've been thinking about that a lot because I really do want to write love songs and lose myself, but I don't know how to do it. There are two competing parts of myself. The one that believes in love and wants to be in on that and wants to write with those feelings, and the person who thinks that those feelings are weak. So that's been my dilemma. I've been thinking about this for a while and there are a lot of examples of women singing heartbreak songs.

**ME:**

How about "I Will Always Love You" by Dolly Parton?

**LAURA:**

That's a good one.

**ME:**

It's strong.

**LAURA:**

But it's like, "I will always love you but I'm leaving you and I'll love you from my tower of strength."

Ultimately, all I want is to believe. I want to believe in that cinematic running-through-the-rain-in-slow-motion feeling. I want to believe in the soaring pop song sentiment, of problems that can be fixed if you can just find the right chord change or metaphor. But there's no getting around the fact that my belief in love songs, while thrilling at times, has more often than not left me haggard and wanting.

The truth is that complications in love rarely come from a person not knowing that someone feels a certain way about them. It's much more intractable than that. Our hearts are set on courses that can perhaps be changed very slightly over the long term with a heavy hand on the tiller, but you can't just turn someone completely around and bring them towards you. At least not with just a song.

That song I wrote for Rachel, about her eyes telling so many wild tales, I once sang to her at a show. Another girl was onstage, singing along with me. Rachel was so angry that she couldn't even speak to me afterwards. Later, she confessed that it hurt her to hear me sing it in another context, this song that was hers. She felt betrayed. "Yes, the song is about you," I said, "but it's also a song that I like to sing and I'm a musician and I have to play shows and find songs to sing and have someone harmonize with me, and if I start excluding songs that are only for certain people in certain contexts then I'm going to run out of songs to play." And so the once-pure intent behind a song comes up against the realities of filling out a setlist.

The burden, I would argue (not that it's a competition), weighs more upon the songwriter than the subject of the song. Even if someone might value, or have once valued, certain songs that I wrote, even valued them so much that there was even a time they couldn't stand seeing me sing them with a different girl by my side, they have the freedom to cast them aside and decide that they no longer mean anything. But I still have to live with those songs. Sometimes, when I'm strumming out those familiar chords, it almost feels like I've gotten divorced and have pulled up outside my unborn child's school, waiting for that first glimpse of that face we created, that constant reminder of love's power and the ache it leaves behind. As I prepare a setlist for a show I have to decide whether or not to sing the song about wanting to believe.

Love songs are probably just selfish acts. We see something in someone else that resonates—"the reflection of what our soul has projected on to them"—and we try to capture that in music. We twirl and spin it into this beautiful cotton candy, full of light and air, but it's still just a confection that will always taste better to us than to them. Every attempt to make it seem noble or pure will end in disappointment.

But I don't know how to stop trying.

Dear __________,

You know what? Fuck love letters. Fuck words trying to describe feelings. How can a word describe a feeling? It weighs it down too much. It's like tying a stapler to a dragonfly. It's like tying a swing set to a moth. Feelings are light. Feelings are pure light, and they want to fly up and frolic. Words are thought-out and laden with meaning and connotations and subtext and double-entendres and what-was-*that*-supposed-to-mean and the more you try to knit them into a pretty little *Home Sweet Home* type of sampler, the more they come out as *Fuck You Forever, Grandma.* You can't help it, because words get away from you and say things you don't want to say. You're just typing along and then the words wake up and say, "Hey, we know what you're trying to say, we got this," and they smirk like a Spring Break date rapist and take over the sentence and you sort of check out and just let them go because hey, they're words, they probably know what's best. Then when you look at the letter days later in your sent folder you see how stupid your words were, but because they were words and not just a painting or something, you're stuck with the concrete finality of them. You said these things. You really said them. You can't take them back. Gah. GAAAH.

Fuck the idea that I can change someone's heart even one percent by writing the perfect letter. I've spent half my year composing a letter in my head to you that would pull you over to my side, to make you understand everything, to make you fall in love with me, and every time I finally try to write that letter it just makes things worse. It's not because love letters are worthless, it's because love letters are too powerful.

Your target is overwhelmed by the thought and consideration put into every sentence, and they begin to realize how they don't put nearly that much thought and consideration into anything regarding you, and so, in a panic, they cut all ties and just bail. When what you really hoped they would do is open the letter and read it carefully and clutch it to their heart and smile fondly and put it on their hope chest or whatever and instantly book a plane ticket or do whatever they have to do to come see you. But they're not actually scouring over every word like they're all vital pieces of nutrition worth soaking up. In fact they're probably just skipping over whole sentences. Whole sentences! Sentences that you agonized over, sentences that took you months to write, trying to find the right words for. They're just scanning over them looking for phrases that stick out. But you weren't writing it to have phrases that stick out. You were writing about your feelings. You're not composing a newspaper headline.

I know this because I've been on the other side. I've been one of those heartless people, and probably will be again. I've received a love letter and known that I couldn't match the feelings of the other person at that time, and I've just squinted at the letter through my hands and hid it away somewhere and never felt strong enough to really read it.

Love letters were never meant to be arguments in a court case, but that's how I've come to see them. After an undeniable string of logic, the jury will have no choice but to conclude that, "Ah, see?

He loves you. Now go with him," and the bailiff will come over and drag you towards a life of making curtains with me while watching *The Daily Show*. What kind of victory would that be, though? Sentenced to be in love? Forced into it through rhetoric and turns of phrase? Where would that get us? I'm just going to have to stop trying to tie the dragonflies and moths down. No more love letters. At least to you. At least now.

Love,
Nick

# *Twenty-five*

It's just a five-minute walk from my room at the meditation center to the dining hall, but each raindrop this morning feels like a little insult. Without an umbrella—or even a windbreaker, for that matter—I'm trying to make my peace with being uncomfortable. Suddenly I hear quick footsteps behind me in the gravel and a teenage boy, the youngest person in the whole retreat, catches up to me, matches my stride, and holds out an umbrella for the both of us. The code of silence forbids even eye contact or gestures, but I hope he can feel my gratitude.

This is the same teenager who was brought to the center by his mom. As the two of them stepped up to the registration table on the first day, the man behind the table with a shaved head and placid expression gazed at them. "Welcome to our center," he said. "We're going to indoctrinate your child into our cult." The mother looked terrified for a second, and finally the man said, "I'm kidding." The mother didn't laugh.

# *How to write a song*

I DON'T OFFER these steps because I consider myself an expert at writing songs. Let's think of it this way. Let's say that there's an Asian grocery store downtown that sells delicious Banh Mi sandwiches for $2.25 and I've been there and you haven't, and the route there is a little complicated, so I've scribbled some directions out for you on the back of an envelope. If you don't follow these steps precisely, you will be forever lost in Chinatown. That's all. But if you think you can get there on your own, by all means.

1. Pick a key. Be considerate of your bandmates' wishes: keyboardists like to play in C. String players like to play in G. Horn players like to play in B flat. So. Let's make it in C sharp. (It's important to stick it to people who want everything to be easy.)

2. Have some novel musical idea, please. Some basic germ of a whim. There are only twelve different notes, so this can be hard.

3. Put your instrument down. Lie on your back and stare at the ceiling for three hours. Three and a half hours. Actually, don't time it. Just stare at the ceiling.

4. Buy a Greyhound ticket. Make it the longest possible journey. If you live in Florida, buy a ticket for Seattle. If you live in Texas, make it for outside of Texas. Sit on that bus. Don't bring an iPod or any music to listen to. Don't bring any books to read. Stare out the window at America. Try to sleep on the metal bar near the window that shoots out cold air. Use your coat as a pillow, even though this will make you cold. Do not extend your body at all beyond the immediate area of your seat. Make no contact with the person sitting next to you. Wherever your bus goes, make sure to get off in Knoxville, Tennessee. Walk past a laundromat that doesn't look like it's still in business, but is. Walk past a Popeyes. Go back to the Greyhound station and stare at the tile grout in the bathroom. Get back on the bus. Ride it to your final destination. Stay at a friend's apartment in that city. Be broke. Buy a can of beans, but don't buy a can opener. Try to figure out how to cook beans without opening the can. Give up. Starve.

5. Pick a subject to write about. There should be plenty to say by now. Settle on one of the following subjects:

a. Falling in love.

b. Falling out of love and tearing up photographs.

c. Being in love with someone who doesn't love you and running through the rain in slow motion.

d. Being in love with someone who recently fell out of love with you while you sit in an apartment with no furniture.

e. The fact that there is rain and that you also feel pain.

f. The fact that you have a desire that is burning like a fire.

g. The fact that you want to find some kind of peace of mind.

h. Actually, none of these are good subjects. Forget about all of these.

6. Find a canal and walk along it until you reach the end.

7. Write out all the lyrics to one of your favorite songs, including all the repeats, the yeahs, the come ons. Throw this away. This is embarrassing.

8. Go for a walk.

9. Take a shower.

10. Turn off the computer. Turn off every appliance in your house. Unplug them all. Take out all the batteries from every electronic device. You want to be the only source of energy in the room.

11. Leave mid-conversation. Walk away from dinner with macaroni stuck on your fork. Ditch civics class before the end of the semester. Quit your softball team before the final inning.

12. Look at a map and wonder what's going on in Ladysmith, Wisconsin. Realize that your imagination will come up with something far more fascinating than the truth.

13. Open to a random page of the dictionary. "Syzygy." Okay, you can't SING that but maybe you can THINK it. And keep it to yourself.

14. Fall in love. Did we not do this already? Fall in love. Make a mistake. Go down the wrong path. Sell out your friends. Embarrass yourself. Burn bridges. Turn yourself inside out.

15. Make yourself dinner. Use a type of mushroom you've never tried. Think about the earth, how dead bodies decompose in the ground and fertilize the plants we eat and how this makes us all necrovores. (That's a word, isn't it? Necrovores?)

16. Pretend you've forgotten how to tell time.

17. Write a song from the point of view of the main character in someone else's song. Write a song as Jolene. Write a song as Joe. Write a song as Jude. Write a song as Driver 8.

18. Write a song from the point of view of Santa Claus, but just talk about the emotions, the burden of the task. Don't talk about elves and presents. Write a song from the point of view of Snoopy. Of Superman. Of God. Describe what you see, how you feel. Describe your relationships, how you're misunderstood.

19. Write a song from the point of view of someone in an extreme situation. Find a strong emotion inside yourself and expand it to a ridiculous degree. Identify with a soldier in the Spanish Civil War, the rain soaking his clothes, the cold cutting through his bones. Imagine yourself the co-pilot of the Enola Gay. Imagine the guilt you'd feel.

20. Think about the sun, and how it burns but doesn't burn up. How it's violent and destructive, and yet the most dependable part of our lives.

21. Make a list of miracles. That ice floats. That giraffes exist. That you were born with organs on the inside of your body. That hair grows out of the top of your head like a wild plant but is somehow soft and delicate. That sound can be encoded onto vinyl and plastic. That cells have a memory. That water is a liquid. That Buddy Holly got to live at all.

22. Write a song not for musicians but for lovers of music. Write a song for the nineteen-year-old girl alone in her attic room, her record collection small but lovingly assembled, brushing her hair after a shower, unable to tell when someone loves her and when someone just desires her. Write a song for people who don't care about key changes or snare sounds. Write a song for people who climb into icy cars at seven-thirty in the morning.

23. Fail at things. Fail at math and science and history. Fail at putting out the garbage, at bringing in the garbage. Fail at giving your dog its medicine. Fail at turning the headlights off. Fail at describing to people what it is you're doing with your life. Fail at asking the cafeteria worker if there are onions in the soup. Fail at removing your shoes in the chancellor's house. Fail at calming down, keeping your hands steady, standing up straight. Fail at taking care.

24. Take things too far. Miss the sarcasm. Shoot a dead horse. Make too many lists, make them too long. Drown yourself slowly.

25. Decide that it's all wrong. Everything. Your email signature, your general wardrobe aesthetic, your favorite Woody Allen film, your openness to French symbolism, your support of socialized health care. Throw away all your possessions. Let people start worrying that you're going to commit suicide.

26. Lie on your bed, on top of your covers.

27. NOW you can write a song. What key did we choose? C sharp? Write a song in C sharp. The good news is that the song you write will always mean more to you than it will to anyone else. That's also the bad news. It's also the good news. Nobody is scrutinizing it. It can be whatever you want it to be. Just don't make it boring. Or: make it boring. Make it the most boring song ever. That would be something.

28. Don't ask for feedback. Don't poll everyone. Maybe it's not in C sharp. Just make a mistake. Make it wrong. You're not running for president.

This is how I write each and every one of my songs. If you want to find your own way there, go ahead. It might be better that way, actually, because then you'll know how to get back. That part I can't help you with.

# *Twenty-six*

Every day is a little more frustrating. Here I am devoting so much of myself to taking this practice seriously while the fidgeter is just fidgeting, never finding a comfortable position or even taking off his jacket, constantly moving around during the time we're supposed to be still. I finally decide to set up a meeting with my teacher Roger. We meet after lunch in his little office. It's hard to feel okay with speaking after so many days without saying a word. I clear the dust out of my throat and thank him for his time and explain that I'm having a problem with one of the other students. "Is there anything you can do?" I ask.

I guess I'm looking for some sort of policing, expecting that he'll figure out who this guy is and have a talk with him. Since I'm not allowed to speak with the other students, he'll need to do it for me.

"You're going to have to deal with distractions while you try to practice this meditation," Roger says. "Outside of this place, the world is going to be full of annoyances. You need to find a way to focus on yourself and not let your mind grab on to what your neighbors are doing."

There was always a moment in my previous experiences with religious or spiritual practices when I was called to do something that just felt wrong. Praying to God, or asking Jesus into my heart always felt like someone was holding my head underwater. The directness and simplicity of being told to solve my own problems is an invitation to take the lid off the sippy cup and sit at the grown-up table.

DEAR __________,

MACHINES ARE BECOMING more human, while simultaneously there is pressure for humans to act more like robots. Like when you call in to an airline or a bank and you have to speak certain commands and it seems to help if you talk slow and stilted like a robot: "CHANGE … MY … RESER-VA-TION … PLEASE." And the machine tries to simulate empathy by saying something like, "I'm sorry, I couldn't hear you." It also happens when you type words into a computer search engine in a way that the computer will understand, as opposed to how you would naturally like to say what you're saying: "frank o'hara having coke text." But until machines can fully understand all of our nuances, we'll keep having to sand off our weird edges.

All of which makes it so much more important to find people who are still interested in being people. That's why I love talking to you on the phone, where I can try out my impression of a lawnmower, and you can tell me about the last hotel room you stayed in and how the manager in the office was a veteran of the Korean War and wore this glass eye and how does a glass eye even work anyway? The sound of your voice, of your laughter, even though it is being transmitted from your machine up to a satellite and back down to my machine, that sound is what connects me to the living world and gives me the courage to battle the robots for another day.

Yours, with real blood pulsing,
Nick

# *Twenty-seven*

THERE'S A SAYING that all you really own is what you can carry off a sinking ship. I've piloted many sinking ships in the name of touring the United States with my band. Many times on the wide-open highways I felt very free, and many times I felt very overwhelmed by the task of organizing everything, playing music that I cared too much about for people who didn't care enough. Plus I was always worried about how to pay for all that gas.

I met the king of freedom in Burlington, Vermont on one of those tours. He needed help putting his raft in the water so he could circumnavigate the world.

My violinist Nathan used to date a literary critic who always received more books in the mail than she could ever hope to review, so her leftovers gave us something to read in our van. One tour, Nathan showed up with a book called *The Happiest Man in the World.* It was about a man named David Pearlman who called himself Poppa Neutrino. As a child, he had been fascinated to learn about how Australian Aborigines would routinely burn their homes and all their possessions so they could avoid being trapped by the past.

Following their example, he named himself after the neutrino, a sub-atomic particle in perpetual motion. He liked to say, "Rent is the thing that beats us." He took the scraps that people left behind, pieces of wood and foam bricks, and fashioned seaworthy rafts out of them. He formed a family band with his wife and kids called the Flying Neutrinos and played in clubs and subway stations around New York. He sailed across oceans on piles of junk. He once dreamed up an unstoppable football play based on secret signals the quarterback could communicate to the receivers while the play was in progress. He tried to get high school and college football coaches to implement it. He followed whims, and if his whims led him to dead ends, he'd abandon everything and sail somewhere else.

We read about Poppa Neutrino like he was a myth, and Nathan used him as inspiration for a fictional deity he called The Traveler King. He mixed in elements of Yacatecuhtli, the Aztec god of travelers, who dressed in colorful feathers and carried around a bundle of sticks. Nathan would spend all day in the van scribbling poems in praise of his deity and at a quiet moment in the evening after a show he'd humbly gather a few people around and read the poems out loud. He shouted lines of praise about "the kabillion-hoofed stallion of the dawn, cackling as he descended like a brilliant meteor," and then, in the spirit of Martin Prechtel (who said that the purest kind of offering is the one which you destroy), he would tear up the poem and throw the pieces into the wind. I always pictured some person in a town like Columbus, Ohio picking up a little scrap of paper the next day that just had some grotesque adverb like "bamboozingly" scrawled on it. Any time we started to have a run of bad luck Nathan would say it was because we hadn't recently made an offering to the Traveler King, and that if we renounced our needs for comfort and possessions we would be rewarded.

The offerings always did seem to lead to good gigs and better luck, whether because there was an honest-to-God deity helping us or just because our collective attitude improved. Before shows, Nathan would walk around whatever city we were in and fill his briefcase with flowers. If it wasn't the right time of year he'd collect feathers. He'd decorate the stage with them and stick them all over our van.

One time we had a gig in Toronto, but didn't have the appropriate paperwork and were turned around at the border. Even though we hadn't spent any time in Canada, we still had to go through United States Customs to get back in the country. They pulled us aside and made us wait in a little room while they inspected our van. When the officer came to tell us we were free to go he said, "Just one question—what's with all the feathers?"

The worst show we ever played was headlining the comedy night at a small club in Chicago. Via email, the owner told me that he liked to have a band follow the comedians. The nights usually went well, he said, and there was a good crowd of people who would stick around to listen to the bands.

We got to the club and set up our gear before the comedians went on. There were maybe five people in the audience, all of whom were comedians waiting to go up and talk. A drunk MC named Junior gave long rambling introductions that went nowhere. The comedians gave long rambling monologues that went nowhere.

"So do you think girl penguins are happy to get menopause? I mean it'd be like you're in the Arctic and whoa! Wait! Here comes another hot flash ... Ah, that was nice ... well, I think they'd like it ... you know, no more periods ... or hormones ... well whatever, it makes sense."

But it didn't make sense. Nothing anybody said made any sense. It's like they had been given a couple boxes of refrigerator poetry magnets and were told to make up stand-up routines from the available words. This went on for two hours. Nobody laughed at any of the jokes. Not even the other comedians. Many of the jokes were so poorly executed that the comedians had to explain afterwards, "That was a joke."

There was a hopeful moment when several people wandered in and said they were looking for the hip-hop open mic. Apparently Junior liked to promote the show as a hip-hop open mic to trick people into coming. After they left, Junior pointed at our musical equipment onstage and said it looked like "Arcade Fire after the rapture."

All night long, Nathan had been writing feverishly on a piece of paper. Finally he asked Junior if he could go up and deliver something. "Is it funny?" Junior asked. "Well, it'll make you laugh," Nathan said. "Is it a poem?" Junior asked. "Well ... no," Nathan said as he looked at the piece of paper he was holding. "It's sort of a ... a tribute ... to our band's deity." Junior was stumped by this and so ceded the microphone to Nathan, who proceeded to give an offering to the Traveler King, right there from that stage with an audience of five terrible comedians. This might not sound blasphemous on the surface, but keep in mind that offerings to the Traveler King had only ever been performed in dark alleyways at two in the morning, around bonfires in front of one or two people, or in empty fields and so on. The offerings were not done for applause, and they were torn up immediately when Nathan was finished reading them. They were solely for the benefit of the Traveler King, who protected us on the road. Doing it onstage into a microphone was a first for Nathan, and even though he was the most entertaining performer on that particular night, funnier than any of those comedians by virtue of being honest, he did feel bad afterwards, as though he hadn't done right by the Traveler King.

The comedians kept going on and on, and we slowly packed up our instruments behind them as they talked, never actually playing a note.

After a few years in my band, Nathan got married and moved to New York. Not only did we now not have someone who would write absurdist poetry and shout it into the air, we also didn't have a violinist who flopped around onstage and caught the audience's attention. His absence left a big hole in the heart of our band and I wasn't sure I could go on without him.

I needed to find a connection to the Traveler King myself, but I knew I couldn't just emulate Nathan. One time in New Mexico we decided that we sorely needed to make an offering to the Traveler King. This would be difficult since it was just me and William and neither of us had done an offering before. We always just watched Nathan read his beautiful poems and then rip them up. We didn't even have an old one we could reuse. We'd have to come up with something new. We stopped in Truth or Consequences and walked down the main street until we found a dried-up old rowboat sitting in a little garden. "Let's do it there," I said. I picked a few desert flowers and we stepped into the rowboat.

"Dear Traveler King ..." I started hesitatingly, clearing my throat, " … aka Papa Hobo ..."

I got no more than a few words further before an old man walked by. "Hey," he said, "there are nails in that rowboat. Be careful."

"Okay," I said, looking down and seeing no nails.

The old man stopped walking and said, "No really, it's dangerous in there."

I honestly thought he was overreacting. "Alright," I said. "We're just making a little offering to the Traveler King."

"You know what? Just get out of that rowboat."

"No it's okay. We're alright." I laughed nervously.

"Look, Silly," he said. "Get out of the rowboat. Now."

He actually called me Silly. I remember that clearly. We slowly stepped out of the rowboat, ending the most pathetic and ineffective offering to the Traveler King ever. But as the old man walked away, William and I grinned at each other. "You know, of course, who that was," I said. "*That* was the Traveler King."

We were driving through Pennsylvania when we saw a sign for the town of Shanksville. We pulled off the highway and visited the memorial to Flight 93, the plane whose hijacking was thwarted by its passengers on September 11th. At the time, the memorial was just a little shelter in an empty field where the plane had crashed. Nobody in the band had expected it to be so humbling to look at a photo of the United States Capitol on the wall with a label under it that said, "The Intended Target."

We got to Burlington a few nights later and were setting up our instruments in the venue when Lee, who owned the place, started chatting with me. He was admiring the photo on the cover of my record *A Narrow Way* and wanted to know more about it. I told him that it was a picture of us playing outside City Lights Books in San Francisco, and I pointed out how you could trace a triangle on it between the references to Jack Kerouac, Lawrence Ferlinghetti, and Allen Ginsberg.

Lee mentioned that Poppa Neutrino was always talking about triads, about how in life your three choices in any situation are to "engage, redirect, or leave." I remembered reading in *The Happiest Man in the World* that Poppa—as he was known to his friends—had learned about Buddhism from Allen Ginsberg himself while sitting in Café Vesuvio, the café where the photograph on my album had been taken. There was a rumor that Poppa sometimes hung around Burlington, so I asked Lee if he'd ever met him. Lee said he had just seen him an hour ago. This gave me the same tingle I had when I was five years old and saw the half-eaten cookies and empty glass of milk on Christmas morning. *He had been in this room.* I asked Lee if he could invite Poppa to the show.

I don't know how to talk about freedom without it sounding like a campaign slogan. "Freedom" is one of those words that has been almost completely soaked through like the cloth on a Molotov cocktail by disingenuous politicians who know that the word stimulates emotions, but who have no interest in helping anyone actually achieve freedom.

Imagine if we grew up only idolizing the people who had attained the most freedom. Actors, politicians, and professional athletes would move towards the bottom of such a list. Despite having a large public forum to speak their minds, they say almost nothing, fearing what might happen if they upset the machinery that gives them this awesome power. It's like having the world's largest megaphone and whispering into it because you're afraid that someone will take it away.

A hero should be a catalyst to get you to think of your life in different terms, not just someone you try to emulate. Poppa Neutrino was my hero, but this didn't lead to me scavenging for junk or sleeping on the streets. Many people who are looking to free themselves often get out of one trap and fall into another. So often, declaring war against society leads to you fighting against your own best interests—your body and spirit. Poppa was more interested in freedom than in tearing anything down. He identified what he called "The Four Jailers:" your landlord, your boss, your mate, and yourself.

We started our set that night in Burlington with no sign of Poppa. He was seventy-seven years old and suffering from congestive heart disease and arthritis, so I began to wonder how realistic it was to think that he'd come to see someone he'd never heard of play music. A few songs in, an old man wearing a poncho entered the club. He was followed by three dogs and two people. They looked like they had stepped out of the Bible, like this was a group that was ready to march across blazing deserts. The old man had an unkempt white beard and wore a scuffed straw hat. He looked like a mixture of a homeless man and a college professor, which I suppose is exactly what he was. He sat in his chair in such a way that his body was facing ninety degrees away from me, like he was taking in the space before he turned his energy to the music.

As I sang each song I focused my words more and more towards him, and he slowly responded by rotating his body, so that by the end of the set I was staring directly into his eyes. After the last song I put down my guitar and walked straight to him. I reached for his hand and said, "It's an honor to meet you." At this point I could have imagined anything happening. Lee had warned me that Poppa could come off as cranky because he would get frustrated when people were not putting their entire focus into interacting with him. Sometimes he would walk out on a conversation when someone was in the middle of a sentence. He certainly wasn't going to make small talk.

I've tried to piece it together exactly in my head, and what he said seems to look best laid out as poetry.

> No, it's an honor to get to listen to your music
> I was at the symphony a few days ago
> listening to Beethoven
> and I was so depressed
> because music has gotten so tired since then

but then coming here tonight
and listening to your harmonies
and your arrangements
I felt my faith in music restored.

After many unfulfilling nights of touring, I felt like I had been jolted by some remarkable new defibrillator that doesn't just save you from dying, but saves you from not fully living.

In the bustle of the crowd, I didn't get to talk to Poppa much more, but Lee announced to the room that Poppa needed help putting his raft in the water the next morning. Even though we were staying an hour and a half outside Burlington, I promised that I would get up early and come back to the city to help out. After all, this was going to be his last voyage, a two-year trip around the entire planet.

Poppa's boat was parked in a residential neighborhood a couple miles from the lake, where he and his friends had worked on it, hammering it into a shape that looked like some sort of bizarre, handmade, Burning Man art piece. I wasn't the only one who had woken up early for this. My bassist William, my drummer Andrew, and my tour manager Lori also couldn't resist the adventure. Despite having been built from mismatched scraps of wood, the boat actually looked more seaworthy than I had imagined it would. But it was obviously the product of necessity and improvisation rather than some well-thought-out plan. The boat was slimmer than previous rafts of his, and it looked like it was built for endurance, long and narrow, less than ten feet wide and maybe fifty feet long. (I thought of Matthew Power's *Harper's* essay about an ill-fated trip down the Mississippi with the anarchist Matt Bullard: "My first impression was of the Unabomber's cabin set afloat.")

We tied rope all around it, about twenty of us, and started pulling. Someone had shoved a few dollies underneath the boat, but those kept slipping out. A kid in sparkly circus attire and big sunglasses played a travel acoustic guitar to encourage us, singing Bob Dylan songs as he weaved through the small crowd. All the songs seemed to be about sailing and goodbyes, one of them with the refrain, "No greater than Jonah, no less than the whale." I hadn't remembered Dylan having so many songs about sailing.

We pulled that boat all the way down North Street and onto Battery, with Poppa Neutrino sitting on top because he lacked the strength to walk as fast as us. The cheap caster wheels disintegrated under the weight, so we had to keep pulling the boat over to the sidewalk and go find more wheels to bolt to the bottom. We trundled down the street, sounding something like an army of skateboarders. We rolled past a graveyard where the young men looked up from their lawnmowers to see what we were doing. Poppa and his crew were handing out Mardi Gras beads to everyone. Three men with big bellies were laughing at us. The one nearest me asked, "What is this, some protest? What are you guys protesting?" I said, "Nah, it's not a protest. He's gonna sail around the world." To which he had no reply.

Maybe it *was* a protest, though, a protest against all the ways that people think you have to behave. No matter how many people die to secure freedom for others, people still look for ways to give up that freedom. So a ragged boat made out of junk with wheels that were tearing apart was a kind of protest against living in that world. After the wheels fell off, the metal braces that held them in place hit the ground and dug into the asphalt. And still we dragged Poppa's boat down the street, leaving our mark along the entire route.

Other people asked if it was a parade. Sure, it was that, too. It was a parade and it was a protest. It was Gay Pride in San Francisco, it was painting faces for the Mardi Gras, and it was launching a man on his last journey, seventy-seven years old and still wanting to see the world. It was hard work. We rested on the side of the road as people in cars gawked at us. Everyone was tired and frustrated about the wheels falling off so Poppa gathered us together for a meeting. We had to lean in close to hear what he had to say because he was old and he talked softly. I thought he was going to offer some plan or tell us all that we had to work harder. Instead he said, "Let's have a party." I went to the store and bought chips and sandwich makings and we sat on the boat in the sunshine waiting until better wheels came. The guitar player seemed to bust in with an appropriate verse any time there was a dip in the energy, like he was our hired traveling minstrel. It was a beautiful day in Vermont, after all, and there was not any particular rush. When someone finally arrived with better wheels, we bolted them on and resumed dragging the boat down the street.

Finally we could see the water, but first we were faced with a steep downhill ramp that led to the boat-launching area. It was too dangerous for Poppa to ride on the boat at this point so he climbed down gingerly. "I never thought my legs would go," he said under his breath. One of his crewmen heard him and said, "What's that, Poppa?" and Poppa repeated, "I never thought my legs would go." His crewman said, "Well, you still got your sea legs, Poppa."

Just then, someone arrived in an old pickup truck. The bumper was falling off, but that was fine. Every solution that day seemed to arrive right at the moment a problem was beginning to feel overwhelming. Our latest helper drove the truck in front of the raft very slowly to support it while we eased it down the hill. When we reached the bottom, we all cheered and pulled the raft across the last hundred yards of the parking lot, ramming it into speed bumps, briefly losing the wheels again, then propping it up and continuing onwards. When we got to the water's edge we tore the rest of the wheels off and laid the boat onto metal pipes, sliding it over those and into the lake.

There was no more help we could give him. We had a show to play that night in Maine. I went up to Poppa Neutrino and shook his hand. I guess when you're saying goodbye to someone you don't ever know for sure whether or not you're going to see them again, but in some cases you know that it's goodbye forever.

Poppa still had something important to do before he could start his journey. A day or two after putting the boat in the water he went to the hospital and had a pacemaker installed. Later that week his surgeons came to the dock to see him off, even though they strongly recommended that he cancel the trip. There probably aren't a lot of seventy-seven-year-olds telling their heart surgeons that they're going to float around the world for two years, but it wasn't crazy to think that he could make it. After all, he had floated down the Mississippi and across the North Atlantic from Newfoundland to France.

"I've lived through levels of fear I never thought I had," he said about that previous Transatlantic voyage. "The waves were so big and so steep, spitting foam across our raft, that I found the coward in myself."

# *Twenty-eight*

Janis Joplin stands in front of her band, wearing green, purple, and pink boas in her hair. "This is a song called 'Get It While You Can'," she says, "because you're gonna *need* it."

She then sings a strong interpretation of Jerry Ragovoy and Howard Tate's gospel-influenced song that wasn't quite a hit a few years earlier. Her energy is a bit too hyper for the looking-back-at-life advice the song gives, and she sometimes changes the chorus to "*Grab* it while you can," but it is a powerful song, and she does it justice. You would never guess that Janis is only twenty-seven years old. She looks like she has been singing and drinking for at least forty years. At the end of the song, Dick Cavett remarks on how she's out of breath. (It's his show, he gets to say what he wants.) Janis, sizzling like bacon, says, "I get so turned on by doing one [song], that it's hard to stop after one, to tell you the truth, because it just makes you want to do more." Less than two months later, she is dead.

At the Montreux Jazz Festival in 1976, eleven years before she dismantles "My Baby Just Cares for Me," Nina Simone is onstage wearing a sleek black dress. She finishes a song at the piano and walks up to a microphone in the center of stage to overwhelming applause. She bows to the audience, gets down on her knees and hangs her head like she is really grateful. The drummer starts playing a quick march and she grabs the mic off the stand and frolics around stage with a mysterious purpose. (Is every performer in the seventies on cocaine?) She sings softly to herself the old prison song "Rosie."

"Be my husband, and I'll be your wife."

She begins to sing louder and more directly into the mic as she moves around the stage.

"Stick to the promise that you made me. Stick to the promise that—" she cuts herself off, and without missing a beat, asks the audience, "—you remember this one? Yeah?"

"You know," she tells them, "I made thirty-five albums, they bootlegged seventy. Oh everybody took a chunk of me."

There are a few chuckles. She looks out at the room, regarding the audience as a group of students that may never understand what she's trying to teach.

"Yesterday," she continues, "I went to see Janis Joplin's film here. And what distressed me the most—and I started to write a song about it, but I decided you weren't worthy, because I figured that most of you were here for the festival and you just really—" she pauses to make a tsk-tsk sound as she looks at the ground.

"Anyway, the point is, it pained me to see how hard she worked, because she got hooked into a thing and it wasn't on drugs." The word "drugs" she speaks with a British accent. "She got hooked into a feeling. And she played to *corpses*." Nina delivers the word "corpses" with wide eyes, like she is talking to three-year-olds about how *we don't hit people, we just don't do that.* She tsk-tsks again. "You know what I mean?" Then she falls back and bursts into laughter, like she's just messing with everyone. "But it's true," she says finally.

What does she mean? Is she saying that Janis was full of life, but wasted her energy on crowds who didn't care? Is that the aspect of Janis she identifies with? Nina goes back to singing the prison song, "If you promise me you'll be my man, I'm gonna love you as best I can. Oh baby, oh baby."

The original version of "Get It While You Can" was sung by Howard Tate, a soul singer who spent time around greatness, but never really hit it big himself. His recording of the song is gritty and deep, helped by a pummeling chorus that speeds up from the verses and features a wall of gospel backup singers. Every time he sings the refrain "get it while you can," he anticipates the downbeat, like he just can't wait to get it out.

Howard toured the circuit for a while, but turned his back on the music business after fellow singer Lloyd Price's manager was killed outside a club in Times Square. Besides, he explained later on, "I wasn't getting any record royalties. So I became a securities dealer with Prudential."

The straight life didn't go any smoother for him. He divorced his wife of two decades a few years after their thirteen-year-old daughter died in a house fire. He lost his home and his job and became addicted to crack, sleeping in New Jersey homeless shelters in the eighties.

Jerry Ragovoy searched for his old friend and collaborator Howard Tate for more than a decade. The liner notes from a 1995 reissue of Tate's recordings speculated that he was probably dead.

"I looked everywhere for him," Jerry said. "I checked all his old haunts and called anyone who used to know him. But no one knew where he was."

A Philadelphia DJ eventually tracked him down. *The New York Times* covered the reunion.

"Mr. Ragovoy received a phone call from a journalist working with a small British blues magazine. Mr. Ragovoy remarked that it was odd that anyone would want to write an in-depth piece about Mr. Tate after all these years, and the journalist replied that Mr. Tate had a dedicated following overseas.

"'I've spent years trying to find him,' Mr. Ragovoy told the journalist.

"'I spoke to him yesterday,' the writer said."

Jerry Ragovoy was predictably stunned: this figure that had begun to seem almost imaginary was now confirmed to exist. They eventually met up and Jerry discovered that Howard's voice was still strong, if maybe a little huskier. They recorded a new album together and set up live shows. This time around, a couple of his shows were caught on film.

Howard Tate has a full band behind him, complete with a horn section. He introduces his signature song by remarking on the commercial failure that musicians are so obsessed with and most audiences can't fully understand.

"In 1967 I made a record, and the record was released all over the world, and it just didn't sell that well. But another young lady came along some years later by the name of Janis Joplin and recorded this same song. And I'd like to do my rendition of it, the original rendition of 'Get It While You Can.'"

His voice is strong as he sings the first verse, but when the band comes in on the chorus, the song feels limp. Instead of speeding ahead like on the recording, everyone is right on the beat, maintaining the tempo of the verses. It all feels a bit too careful, like a slow dance at a high school homecoming.

Luckily, there's a different, much more devastating version of the song. Jerry himself accompanies Howard on piano. They're in Paris on the same tour, but this time there is no band, no backup singers. The tempo of the song is slower than the original and never speeds up. The choruses—which in the original were triumphant—are now heartbreaking. Although Howard sticks close to the original lyrics and inflections of the song, it's impossible not to feel like he's looking over the audience in front of him wondering what could have been. After decades away from the stage, he seems grateful to be in front of anyone at all. He doesn't look like he wants to fight the audience, or teach them something. He just looks like he wants us to understand where he's been, and that even if it's too late for him, there's still time for us.

"Get it while you can. I want to tell you tonight, to get it while you can," he sings.

At the end of the song, Jerry lifts his hands from the piano for just a moment. Into the silence, like it's the *amen* of a sermon, Howard says, "Don't turn your back on love."

Dear __________,

What is the proper amount of love to feel for someone in a romantic situation?

Is it best to fall down the slope and into the lake, to be completely consumed and in love with every aspect of their person, to enjoy their face and their smell and their voice and their everything? Because I've done that, and it left me with a split-open shoe flapping on the sidewalk as I walked down 16th Avenue. I wanted to step in front of a bus to relieve the pain.

Or is it better to always hold yourself tightly, to be skeptical of dramatic gestures, to drag your feet as you're pulled into some adventure, to scoff and judge and be quiet and removed? Because I've done that too, and it left me kicking wound-up sheets off my bed while sleeping alone in the hot August night.

There is no proper amount.

I'd rather think of all the ways that we are immortal:

When we have a great night in that bar in a tiny town in the mountains, when we laugh and sing and dance, and that night becomes part of a story, part of the legend of that place and a way of living.

When we sing together and our voices match up like a lock in a key, the teeth of my voice fitting with the tumbler of yours.

When we look up in the sky and realize that we are made from stars and that starlight will travel forever, or at least until it finds some eyeball somewhere to give its image.

When we let go of the particulars of our personality and our ego enduring, and realize that the experience of experiencing the world as ourselves is a relatively short one, but the experience of just being a part of everything never ends, and that's not sad or painful or anything, it just is, and it's okay.

When we love something, and that love goes out infinitely in every direction, even if it's a love that we have to keep quiet, because the bridge between us has been so burned that we can't trust walking over it anymore. Even then. Even if it's a quiet, quiet love that we whisper only to ourselves as we chase fireflies, the lit ones always just over there.

Yours literally forever,
Nick

# *Twenty-nine*

ON THE LAST full day of the retreat our teachers introduce a new kind of meditation that is focused on not just healing ourselves, but spreading that feeling outside of our bodies. It ends with Goenka singing a repetitive chant, and saying over and over again, very gently, "Be happy." As the song keeps going you can hear him step away from the microphone, his voice fading out. "Be happy. Be happy."

I used to be scared that if I lost my sadness I would lose an important part of myself. I think I was just afraid to push against all of the momentum of that imploding melancholy, as beautiful and noble as it seemed. You really do *have* to be happy, no matter how uncool it sounds.

Many times during meditation, I've found myself thinking about all the people I know who are trapped in some way. I've thought about all the men I met at Folsom Prison earlier in the year, and how they are all still sitting in the same rooms in which I left them. They'll be in those rooms for many years, some of them for the rest of their lives. Their suffering is everywhere in the world, in and out of prison. It's what originally drew me to music: to calm some of that suffering, at least for myself, and maybe in other people.

When the song and the session end, I start crying and don't stop for twenty minutes. I cry for this man who put so much effort into telling people to be happy. I cry for how hard it has been in my life to just do that, that even though I am in my mid-thirties I still haven't figured it out. I cry for the moments I never fully enjoyed because I thought I had to be separate from them, observing them in some secret way. I cry for the times I wasn't present, off thinking about the past or the future. I cry for all the times I've been rejected, all the people I've loved that didn't want to see me, all the success I wanted but could never find. I cry for all the ways I've locked myself up in different bedrooms in different houses, afraid to go out in the world, feeling like I could never belong. I cry for how hard it has been for me to just feel like a person.

Eventually I get to my feet. Maybe some of the childhood feelings that were deep in my cells came out in the salt of those tears. Maybe all that shit could just disappear. Oh, if I could just set it all on fire and walk away, escape the pull of gravity, and steal my way around the world.

All the other students have long ago left the hall. A sign outside the door explains that the code of silence has now been lifted. All the silent nondescript people I've spent the last ten days with suddenly have names and faces and look so alive. It's amazing how much the lack of language quiets a personality. Even the fidgety guy is now a person, though I still don't want to talk to him. Everyone is laughing, sharing stories about how hard it has been and what they have gotten out of it. I go into the dining room with everyone and pour myself a hot mug of Inka. Posted to the bulletin board is Goenka's obituary. He died just a couple weeks ago.

It feels like I've been shaken out of a dream. All around me people are exchanging stories from the past ten days: the insomnia, the rain, the difficulties in concentrating. I sit at a table warming my hands around the mug. I am not ready to talk to anyone else, to go back to the world of language defining everything. I retreat to my room, alone. I don't want to hear *Graceland* or any other music. I want this silence to linger.

These are the first words I write: "Decide to love the things that make you sad. Love change and chaos. Love discomfort and awkwardness. Find one thing in all of that to love."

# *Thirty*

I AM IN A SMALL BAR in Bogotá, Colombia watching a guy named Gabe play music. My editor Michael put me in touch with him, describing him as a "talented musician, total weirdo, worth your time." I came here after the meditation retreat to get some writing done in a country I can afford.

There are maybe three other people here. Gabe is holding a kora, a West African instrument that has a globe at the bottom, a long neck, and a bunch of strings connected to leather straps. He has a small tambourine tied to his knee that he can shake rhythmically. He plays his first song and the notes cascade out kind of like a harp, with unique patterns and rhythms. He plays the rhythmic part then solos over it, and with the tambourine and his voice the band is complete.

I have seen people play the kora before, but always in traditional ways, very respectful of the heritage of the music. Gabe is writing his own songs on it and singing "Summertime" in Spanish. At the table next to me is Gabe's dad, visiting from Chicago. It's not hard to discern the disappointment of a parent who is wondering how his child is ever going to survive if his is playing shows in Colombia on some strange West African instrument to four people.

After Gabe finishes his set I turn to his dad and try to make conversation. "What do you think?" I am asking what he thinks of Bogotá, but he thinks I am asking about his son's music. "I think he's a starving artist," he says.

There are a couple things I hear in a statement like that. One of them, of course, is a deep love of a father for his child. He went through the sleepless years of creating this human being and worrying about his child's survival. It's hard to turn around and accept that you can't always keep your child from harm, or poverty.

Yet the other thing I hear in "starving artist" is a kind of abdication of humanity in favor of capitalism.

The life I found myself in after years of playing music was what I would refer to as a lottery mentality. I was living in Portland, a city full of ambitious musicians. There is unfortunately no middle class in the music business like there was a generation ago when, as a competent band providing a night of music at a bar, you could get paid decently. Now you are either one of a few dozen to have a meteoric rise, another several hundred who have found a niche through hard work and luck, or you are one of the millions who work in near obscurity and poverty. There is no shame in being obscure, but there is a shame in living your life under the constant delusion that everything will be better once your ship comes in. As John Steinbeck wrote, "Socialism never took root in America because the poor see themselves not as an exploited proletariat, but as temporarily embarrassed millionaires."

I found myself, along with many of my friends and peers, constantly dissatisfied with how my music was received, but still determined to do what it took to improve my chances the next time around. That started to shift when I finally began to ask myself honestly, "What if it will never improve? What if I will never sell more albums, play to bigger crowds, have any bigger success?" If the answer to that question was anything short of, "I'm perfectly fine with that," then I realized I needed to reorder my priorities.

It turned out I wasn't okay with my life as I was living it. My happiness was unduly affected by the lack of a positive Pitchfork review. I played music because I loved music and my dreams of success were shaped by the examples I saw around me, and not achieving that success naturally felt like a failure. Not just that but it felt like I had been wrong about what I thought I loved, like I had been caring deeply about a woman who turned out to be just a pillow on a mop handle.

So I had to ask myself, "What parts of my world can I control that reliably make me happy?" Record reviews and show attendance aren't things I can actually control, but it is always within my control to learn new skills. This led me to New York, where I studied ballet music and opera. It led me to take drum lessons to understand rhythm in my body and not just my mind. I was no longer deferring my happiness to some imagined period when the acclaim would come and I would finally reach the level of success I thought I deserved.

It brought me through ten days of silence and finally here to Bogotá, where I am trying to fall back in love with music. It feels good, watching Gabe hold that strange instrument that is half furniture and half conversation piece, and seeing him make really wonderful sounds from it. Any time you live a life according to what you think someone else wants from you, whether it's your parents or society or God, you are going to come up disappointed. That doesn't mean that you have to run away to Colombia and play the kora. It might not involve running at all, or music, or art, or anything like that.

If I opened a restaurant and created dishes that I really believed in and put all my love into, I sure hope I wouldn't look across the street at a McDonald's and despair at how much more popular their restaurant was. Even though we were both ostensibly making food products for people to eat, we would be in different universes. I couldn't possibly gauge my success against theirs.

When I first started writing songs all I could dream was that I could make one person somewhere feel not so alone. Writing a song you're really proud of is like making one great dish and then thinking, "How can I get this into the hands of every person on Earth?" The things you'd have to compromise to make that a reality would change the essence of the original. Capitalism tells us that the song you wrote for one person should be heard by ten thousand or it won't really count.

After the show, Gabe invites me to come visit him and his girlfriend and their new baby out at her grandmother's house in the village of Tunja, high up in the mountains outside of Bogotá. And so we've all come out here. Gabe's dad, too.

Last night, we went out into the town square. Christmas was just a couple days ago, so there are still all these flashing lights everywhere attached to little booths offering different treats. There was one kiosk made out of recycled plastic bottles that had a projector casting animated pictures on the ground. Little kids were trying to jump on the images, thinking they'd be able to grab them, but even though they kept coming up empty-handed, they were laughing the whole time. As I was watching the kids I heard a strange sound behind me. Gabe was staring intently into his dad's eyes. Then his dad slumped in Gabe's arms and started making a sound I've never heard a human make before. It was the sound of the body as a malfunctioning machine. I went over to help, but didn't know what to do. He kept making this horrible sound, like the worst snoring you've ever heard mixed with a security system failing. I thought that I was watching someone die right in the middle of town square a couple nights after Christmas.

Gabe kept saying, "You're okay, Dad. It's okay." It turns out that Gabe's dad has epilepsy, and a combination of the flashing lights and the altitude might have set him off. He has fits like this as often as twice a week, and one time it happened on the platform of the 'L' in Chicago and his body fell on the train as it sped by, breaking his arms and legs.

Once I knew that he wasn't dying, the image of Gabe holding his dad in his hands looked tender to me, especially after his dad had bemoaned his son being a starving artist. Often people have the harshest criticism for other people who are claiming the freedom that they are afraid to claim for themselves.

I know that Gabe isn't the kind of guy who would ever change just to please his dad. He has lived the past three years in Paraguay, and when I asked him what it was like there he told me, "It's amazing. There's just nothing there. You can live on just a few dollars a week."

I keep thinking of the way he described that country. "There's just nothing there." He said those words with a wonder in his eyes about something that most people would be bored with. It is the first time that a description of such a place excites me. Empty places used to make me sad, because there wasn't the spectacle of human fireworks to distract me from my longing. Now when I think of empty spaces I think of having room to work out song lyrics, or read about sailing. Or just spend time in my own brain, which isn't such a terrible place. A small victory that sitting silent for ten days brought me.

Tonight, Gabe has another gig, and so I'm sitting alone in another little bar, when suddenly he comes over to my table and asks if I'll back him up on drums. Gabe knows plenty of crowd-pleasing Colombian favorites like "El Año Viejo" and "Egoísmo." I barely manage to keep the rhythm together, struggling on a foreign instrument in a foreign town. Halfway through the set he starts to play a Spanish-language version of "I Will Survive." I steel myself in the long intro buildup to the song, preparing to bust into a solid disco beat and keep it going until the song ends. I think back to what my drum teacher said: if you put the rhythm in your body and not your head, sit in that groove like it's carved deep into wood and just move in that space, every beat will be in time.

Dear __________,

I won't send you this letter. You wouldn't want to read it anyway. All the letters I've ever written to you were meant to sway your heart in some way. It's hard to think of what I'm trying to do with a letter if it's not to try to sway your heart. It's hard to think of what I'm trying to do with a song if you're never going to hear it.

For so long you defined the shape of my love. I pinged signals off of you and knew where you were. After a few pings went unanswered, it was too hard to think of sending out orphaned pings into the blackness.

So I won't send this letter. I won't send any of them. I'll write letters to other people and I'll actually send them, but those letters will all have much lower stakes. I'll talk about trivialities when all I want is to walk down the street pushing bikes with you in a light Portland drizzle, our shoulders close enough to touch when our strides conflict. I want to talk with you about where we go when we die, about what the characters wanted in that movie we just saw. I want to stretch out on a foam pad in the back of my van with you and just wonder.

One time long ago we lay in bed together and I looked at you and said, "Thank you." And I truly meant it. I have trouble expressing gratitude, not because I don't feel it, but because I get afraid that my expression will sound inadequate, and so I end up not making any expression at all.

I want to say thank you again. I love your heart and your eyes, which tell so many wild wild tales. Thank you for being a person and fighting, sometimes with me, sometimes against me. It's all the same fight. Sometimes I get confused which side I'm supposed to be on.

Still, love,
Nick

# *Thirty-one*

The older I get, the more I want to talk with everyone about coincidences. I've noticed that when people are confronted by coincidences they sometimes get defensive, as if by acknowledging them they are confirming a belief in a higher power and that denying them means that the world is a random place where nothing means anything. Really all I want to do when faced with a remarkable wave of coincidences is step back as though from an abstract painting, grab the forearm of the person next to me, feel the texture of their sleeve and say, "Wow. Look at that. Just look."

A few weeks after dragging Papa Neutrino's boat through Burlington, our tour was winding through the garlic fields of Central California. In the van, glancing at the map, I realized we were just a few miles from the San Juan Bautista Mission. I told my bandmates I needed a few minutes to check on something. I paid five dollars to enter the new gift shop at the mission and looked all over but couldn't find the abalone cross I had dug up in that well all those years before. In the parking lot outside the mission, Stelth told me that if I could get a picture of the cross, he'd make a duplicate and swap it with the real one. I told him that I had never considered stealing anything, but I would make an exception for that cross. In reality we both knew it would never happen. We hung out in the courtyard of the mission talking about scams while Stelth taught us how to catch a chicken. "You wave a stick to get its attention, then you draw a line in the dirt and it'll follow it right into your arms."

Every day in every part of the world, there is a bunch of stuff that happens that has no narrative arc, no synchronicity. We are all just shuffling along through the dim avenues of our lives. What distinguishes us from a bear fishing for salmon in the river, ignoring the flecks of gold that only make the fish harder to see? As humans, as beholders of wonder, as seekers of beauty, we have the opportunity to move through this world like miners in old California panning for gold, sifting through dirty river water looking for little glints in the sunlight. We have the power to collect beautiful objects and make them into something bigger, and that is what I mean by appreciating coincidences.

Most people don't know that J.D. Salinger had the first few chapters of his incomplete *Catcher in the Rye* manuscript on him as he stormed the beaches of Normandy on D-Day. Even the most inevitable-seeming things could have been upended by a wayward bullet. It's terrifying to think of in retrospect, this young man carrying sentences that would change so many lives through a battlefield. What would have taken its place, had he been killed? Would anything?

That night, getting ready to play at the Crêpe Place in Santa Cruz, I read online that Poppa and his crew had only made it a few miles into the channels south of Lake Champlain when a big storm hit, thrashing the little boat. They had to duck into a cave and wait out the storm, but the waves pounded the boat against the rocks and completely destroyed it. "The vessel was everything I wanted it to be," Poppa later told the *Burlington Free Press*. "I told the Coast Guard people it was unsinkable. They said, 'Never say that.'"

For Poppa Neutrino, a man who had committed his life to freedom, it must have been a humiliating end to what he thought would be an epic journey. Fifty police and rescue workers came to pull him and his crew out of the sinking ship. He spilled dozens of gallons of gas in the lake, something he apologized for and pledged to clean up.

"We gave everything we had for this one project," he told the paper. "Something will come of it. We all sin. And if we're truly sincere, we can be forgiven." When asked what he needed now, he said, "I need a van. I need a van to sleep in."

A few months later he died of heart failure in New Orleans. Friends and family threw him a small jazz funeral in the streets and spread his ashes in the Mississippi River.

I'll remember Poppa standing on that dock above Lake Champlain at the beginning of another voyage, and I'll remember walking back through the streets of Burlington, stepping over the grooves the boat had carved in the asphalt. The fire department was flushing out all the fire hydrants that day, and water flooded the streets. It soaked our feet and sloshed against the wheels of my van as we got in. My drummer Andrew sat in the front seat. He was a big Bob Dylan fan, so I asked him to put the iPod on for the ride to Maine.

"What album has all those Dylan songs about sailing that that guy was playing today?" I asked him.

"That wasn't Dylan," he said. "I don't know where those songs came from."

# Acknowledgments

Thank you to Michael Heald for asking me to write a book, believing that I could write that book, giving feedback when I was writing a bunch of meandering crap, and turning my words into a real book. I'm so grateful.

Thank you to Stelth Ulvang for being a great friend and staying up late to talk about girls, and for reading drafts of my book faster than anyone else and giving feedback almost immediately.

Thank you to Meghann McCracken for so many intelligent conversations at odd hours, for pushing me to have more empathy for the people I was depicting in this book, to see all sides with fairness.

Thank you to Dave Depper for the unwavering desire to understand how to love everything and for offering early encouragement.

Thank you to Casey Jarman for championing my writing from early on.

Thank you to Lori Englert, Jenn Marino, and David Trisko for reading early drafts of this book.

Thank you to all the people whose conversation and advice inspired me in writing this book: Laura Gibson, Matt Dabrowiak, Chris Cromwell, Nathan Langston, Norah Hoover, Caitlin Gutenberger, Corinne Wolcott, Wilson Vediner, Esme Boyce, CJ Levine, Melissa Wilson, Michael Hebb, Michael Leahy, Michelle Christiance, Mike Midlo, Mont Chris Hubbard, Nanceportation, Burr Datz, Daniel Cooper, Daniel Talsky, Taylor Ross, Dawndae Hamilton, Tatiana Sakurai, Erin Howe, Eric Schmidt, Gabriel Goldstein, Sarah Riddle, Gennie Patterson, Gill Landry, Heather Campbell, Ingrid Langston, Ty Holter, Ural Thomas, Willa Conway, Jamie Stillway, Jasmine Ash, Jenny Logan, Sarah DeCoux, Jesse Elliott, Lindsay McWilliams, Talia Gordon, Peter Walters, Rachel Blumberg, Troy Schumacher, Rick Shaw, Thomas Patterson, Rob Jones, Lisa Wells, Lynnae Griffin, Madeleine Joyce, Sarah Cawley, Marcus Reynolds, Mark Wald, Maryia Martineau, Jesse Hermreck, Ryan Sollee, Samantha Parton, Xan Roberti, Joan Hiller, Joel Kraft, Jolie Holland, Nico Alexander, Steve Otis, Olivia Pepper, Skyler Norwood, Paloma Young, Julie Odell, Karla Starr, Kathleen Duffy, Sarah Fischer, Katie Walenter, Kelsey Bowe, Laura Freeman, Lee Howard, Madeleine Sanford, Leesa Andolaro, Lesli Yazzie, Alexandra Duchene, Sarah Law, Manuel Vignoulle, Pearl Rasmussen, Peter Murray, Zoe Boekbinder, Alejandro Rueda, Daniel Paniagua, Daniela Guzmán, Eric and Anna Bergman, Melanie Brown, Luke Allen, Leah Walbourne, Alea Joy, Amber Padgett, Ashley Edwards, and so many others whose names I never even got.

Thank you to all the people that have been a member of my band, if even for an evening: Nathan Langston, Scott Magee, Sean Flinn, Jason Leonard, John Whaley, William Joersz, Dave Depper, Stelth Ulvang, Matt Dabrowiak, David Williams, Danah Olivetree, Dorota Szuta, Lauren Jacobson, Richie Greene, Andrew Zilar, Max

Barcelow, Macon Terry, Blake Stepan, Griffin Snyder, Stoo Odom, Anthony DeCuccia, Joseph McGinty, Matt Berger, Ryan Dobrowski, Papi Fimbres, Edward Cameron, Dan Hunt, Levi Cecil, Paul Alcott, Tony Schatz, Bonnie Gregory, Esme Patterson, Kaylee Cole, Annalisa Tornfelt, Tahoe Jackson, Laura Gibson, Ali Ippolito, Sarah Fennell, Alex Galt, Dustin Hamman, John Reski, Thomas Paul, Louis Macfarland, Sam Coe, Sean Hayashi, Amanda Lawrence, Amanda Spring, Amanda Kitchens, Victor Nash, Wilson Vediner, Wilson Marks, David Moss, Anna Schott, David Lord, Rebekah Durham, Amanda Stark, Ryan Satterfield, Gavin Bowes, Luzelena Mendoza, Shenandoah Davis, Jonathan Sielaff, Ethan Demarest, Chris Johnedis.

Thank you to John Shepski and Chad Lanning at my record label Fluff & Gravy for being so supportive. Thanks to Kevin Draper at Satellite Collective for giving me a reason to learn more. Thanks to Rick Castaneda for being the easiest person to work with.

Thank you most of all to Carol and Richard Dabrowiak for creating me and having patience while I sorted some things out. Let's go sailing.

Nick Jaina was born in Sacramento. He has released a handful of albums and written the music for several ballets, contemporary dance pieces, feature films, and plays. Go to nickjaina.com for tour dates and information about hosting a live performance.